A Practical Guide to Creating Quality Exams

Quality Exams

by J Balogh, PhD

Published by Intelliphonics, LLC
P.O. Box 4102
Menlo Park, CA 94026

ISBN: 978-0-9973617-0-4

Library of Congress Number: 2016903523

Printed in the United States of America
First edition

Table of Contents

CHAPTER 1:

Introduction

Benefits of Reading This Book

The purpose of this book is to help academic instructors and teaching assistants create quality exams. The benefits are significant and straightforward. With better exams, instructors can improve teaching, more accurately assess student knowledge, reduce student complaints, and avoid lawsuits.

A quick overview of how to develop effective tests is needed because professors and TAs are hired or admitted into their departments because of their expertise in their fields, and most are simply never exposed to testing theory and its applications. I certainly never was, and yet as a teaching assistant, I was given the responsibility of creating exam questions and scoring exams for hundreds of students. I could have benefited from a bit of knowledge about testing at that time. And I believe other teachers feel the same.

Now, more than a decade later, after receiving postdoctorate training in tests and measurements and working in the field of assessment for over 10 years, my goal is to transfer my knowledge of testing to enable anyone in an academic environment responsible for assessing students to create the best exams possible.

Granted, this is not the first book ever published on the topic. However, most books on the subject are written as lengthy textbooks costing hundreds of dollars. Many of these textbooks include prescriptive advice often without ever explaining why the advice is sound. In contrast, this book is specialized for its purpose – to help busy academics who most likely want to know why the guidelines in this book are worth following. As such, it is succinct so that the concepts can be understood quickly and applied in a practical way; and it provides reasons and evidence behind the guidelines. You can also get free online supplementary material. Just visit the following website:

www.intelliphonics.com/source/resources.html.

You have lectures to give and papers to write, so let's get started!

Goal of Testing

In higher education, the main purpose of an exam is usually to determine a student's level of mastery of the material and skills covered in a course. Although tests can be used for many other reasons (licensure, placement, progress monitoring), the focus of this book will be on measuring content mastery, with the ultimate goal of assigning grades.

With content mastery as the focus, the requirements of a test are quite simple. First, the test needs to include relevant material and skills from the course. Second, it needs to be able to discriminate between those students who have acquired knowledge, skills, and abilities from those students who have not. Third, it needs to be consistent and award the same grade to the same person without fluctuations. Finally, it needs to be fair. This book will help you understand these requirements and help you meet them. In a survey of testing ability, Pigge and Marso (1988) found that "teachers, principals and supervisors each rated the adequacy of teachers' testing and evaluation skills below average." It is now time to shatter these perceptions.

CHAPTER 2:

What Makes a Test Good?

There are three essential factors that contribute to how good or bad a test is. These factors apply to all tests regardless of whether they are large-scale standardized tests or small custom tests created for your course. The three factors of good quality are validity, reliability, and fairness.

How do we know that these factors are important? Well, three professional organizations came together to define formal criteria for developing tests and testing practices (among other things). The three organizations were the American Educational Research Association (AERA), the American Psychological Association (APA), and the National Council on Measurement in Education (NCME). These sponsoring organizations published a book entitled *Standards for Educational and Psychological Testing* (2014), referred to as the *Standards*. In the *Standards*, the three concepts that are defined as foundational for testing are validity, reliability, and fairness.

The authors of the *Standards* fully acknowledge that many of the practices described in the *Standards* are not feasible in the classroom because, after all, instructors are not publishing their tests for public use; however, the authors do state that "the core expectations of validity, reliability/precision, and fairness should be considered in the development of such tests" (p. 183).

The concepts of validity, reliability, and fairness will be described below in more detail as they relate to tests in a classroom setting.

Validity

According to the *Standards* (AERA, APA, & NCME, 2014), validity is "the degree to which evidence and theory support the interpretations of test scores for proposed uses of tests." In other words, validity is how well a test is measuring what it is intended to measure. For example, if you are planning to measure students' knowledge of Physics and you give students a test about Philosophy, clearly you cannot make conclusions about the students' understanding of Physics from the test scores. In this case, the test lacks evidence of validity.

The formal definition in the *Standards* is a bit long and seeming circuitous because assessment professionals think that it is misleading simply to say, "Test X is valid." First, the test is a vehicle for helping you to understand what is inside your students' heads. It is not really the test that is of interest, but rather the test scores. In fact, it is not even the test scores themselves that you should be concerned with, but rather the meaning underlying those scores. That is why the formal definition refers to *interpretations* of test scores. Second, testing professionals also believe that it is not responsible just to *declare* that something is valid. It is more scientific to consider evidence. So when they talk about validity, they discuss the quantity and quality of evidence that supports interpreting test scores for an intended purpose.

Regardless of these nuances in the definition of validity, the point is that validity is a critical factor when determining whether or not a test is of good quality, and this concept applies to any test and to any score user, regardless of whether that person is an assessment professional or a classroom instructor.

Validity

"Validity refers to the degree to which evidence and theory support the interpretations of test scores for proposed uses of tests. Validity is, therefore, the most fundamental consideration in developing tests and evaluating tests."

- AERA, APA, & NCME, 2014

Construct Validity

There are different kinds of validity evidence. One kind that is relevant for academic exams is how well the test is measuring the construct of interest. A *construct* is a mental concept or characteristic, such as "achievement in basic chemistry." Unfortunately, a construct is not something physical that you can measure with a ruler or weigh on a scale. Instead, you have to probe what is inside your students' heads indirectly by having them answer questions, write essays, or perform tasks. What becomes tricky is determining whether or not the things you are asking your students to do for an exam will actually be measuring the construct. For the most part, you will be interested in measuring achievement of skills and knowledge in a specific content domain – that's your construct. Common ways of measuring academic achievement are selected-response tests (e.g. multiple choice) and essays. These approaches are widely accepted, so you can rest assured that partaking in the tradition of administering these types of exams does not degrade construct validity in any way.

However, problems can arise when a test does not sufficiently measure a construct. For example, if a test is intended to measure driving ability but includes only a written component, then the test is not measuring the individual's skill of actually driving a moving vehicle. The test suffers from *construct underrepresentation,* which means the construct is not fully addressed by the test. The content of the topics covered in a driving class may be well represented on the written test, but the written test by itself will still lack evidence of construct validity without a performance component. In some cases, a multiple choice exam may not be able to show what a student knows and is capable of as well as an essay. Selection of the style of test can influence evidence of construct validity.

Content Validity

Another kind of validity evidence is based on test content. Is your test covering the right material? Many students challenge exams that do not reflect what was covered in class or what the professor conveyed were the most important concepts. These exams lack evidence of content validity, which is a legitimate complaint. Fortunately, it is a problem that can be avoided.

Thankfully, you can make good decisions during the test-development process that can help you avoid threats to both construct and content validity. The steps covered in this book will help you to gather evidence of validity for your test.

Sensitivity

The quality of the items in a test impacts validity. If the exam is riddled with ambiguous questions that high-performing students get wrong and low-performing students get right, then the test is measuring something different than the material covered in the course, and the test will lack evidence of validity.

The test needs to be able to identify correctly those students who have mastered your content and distinguish them from those students who have not. In the medical field, this concept of measuring the degree to which a test can correctly identify something of interest is called *sensitivity*. Of course, the term is mostly used for tests that can correctly detect a disease or medical condition. (Technically, sensitivity is the proportion of correct positives identified by a test.) But the concept extends to educational testing as well. Which students should pass, and which students should not? When trying to distinguish student ability along a continuum, we refer to a test's (or item's) ability to *discriminate*. The goal is to discriminate high-performing students from low-performing students and everyone in between.

In sum, a test that has sufficient evidence of validity will cover the appropriate content; it will do so in a relevant way; and it will be able to discriminate students who have mastered the content from those who have not. The steps in this book can help you meet these criteria by guiding you to choose the appropriate style of test (Chapter 3), to create a test blueprint (Chapter 4), to write good items (Chapter 5) and to analyze the performance of the test items (Chapter 9).

Reliability

Another indicator of test quality is reliability. Reliability is how consistent test scores are. Ideally, if a student gets an A on your exam on Monday, then the student should get an A on Tuesday (assuming that the student's knowledge of the material remains constant). Granted, the student might not get an A on Tuesday for a variety of reasons that have to do with the student's internal mental state, such as not getting enough sleep or being distracted by an upcoming vacation. But assuming that the student's knowledge of the material is constant *and* the student is in an identical mental state on both days, scores could still be different due to measurement error inherent in the test itself. Some tests are just more reliable than others.

How can you increase reliability? The answer is to add more items. Test length is intimately linked to reliability. A test with only a few items can gather only a small amount of information regarding what the student does and does not know. A test with more items or questions allows you to gather more information, and therefore, the test will most likely be more reliable. In fact, there is a mathematical relation between the number of items a test has and the reliability of that test (Brown, 1910; Cronbach, 1951; Spearman, 1910).

Every test will be different, but generally speaking, I have come across tests with 20-30 items that have reliabilities in the 0.60s and 0.70s, tests with 50 items with reliabilities in the 0.80s, and tests with 100 or more items with reliabilities in the 0.90s. These are just generalizations. There are ways to calculate reliability to check what the specific reliability of your test is (see Appendix A).

Standards for Reliability/Precision

"Appropriate evidence of reliability/precision should be provided for the interpretation for each intended score use."

- AERA, APA, & NCME, 2014
Standard 2.0

In addition to the number of items on a test, another factor influencing reliability is consistency in scoring. This issue arises most when scoring essays in which the amount of credit given depends on the scorer's subjective judgment. The scorer could be inconsistent and assign a paper an A one day and the same paper a B the next day. Also, if multiple people are scoring a test, two graders could potentially provide different scores for the same response. All these differences within individual graders and between graders can compromise the reliability of a test.

There is actually a significant amount of interplay between reliability and validity. Basically, no matter how much work you invest in ensuring that the content of the test matches your content domain and that the tasks are measuring the construct of interest, if your test cannot produce consistent scores, then your test will lack evidence of validity. You cannot have a valid test with low reliability. In another scenario, you could have a test with extremely high reliability, but this does not guarantee that the test is valid. You need evidence of both validity and high reliability for a test to be considered of good quality.

The take-away regarding reliability is that an exam needs to have enough items to provide a sufficient amount of information about the student's mastery of the content to ensure consistency in scoring.

Fairness

The third factor related to the quality of test scores is fairness. Fairness is a student's basic right. If tests or even individual items are biased against (or for) a person or subgroup and this difference is not related to what is being tested, then some may consider the test to be unfair. The technical term for this is *construct-irrelevant variance,* meaning there is extra noise in the test scores caused by something other than the skills and knowledge you are trying to measure.

Standards for Fairness

"Test developers are responsible for developing tests that measure the intended construct and for minimizing the potential for tests' being affected by construct-irrelevant characteristics, such as linguistic, communicative, cognitive, cultural, physical, or other characteristics."

- AERA, APA, & NCME, 2014
Standard 3.2

For example, a test may include items that reference a topic that is taboo for a specific subgroup of students (e.g., a feminist student may be offended by items depicting gender stereotypes such as a woman doing housework and a man going to an office), and this taboo content may distract a student and contribute to a missed correct answer. When this happens, the test has introduced construct-irrelevant variance.

Threats to Fair and Valid Interpretations of Test Scores

"... test content or situations that are offensive or emotionally disturbing to some test takers and may impede their ability to engage with the test should not appear in the test unless the use of the offensive or disturbing content is needed to measure the intended construct."

- AERA, APA, & NCME, 2014

Another example of potential bias is when items include unduly complicated language beyond the technical vocabulary needed for content mastery. In this case, the item is not only measuring knowledge of the content domain but also proficiency in the English language. In some cases, these kinds of items might be biased against non-native speakers.

Fairness also includes providing a comfortable testing environment and appropriate accommodations for students with documented disabilities. Usually, guidelines provided by your institution can help you navigate these situations, but general awareness of these topics can help you to know what to expect.

Overall, there are steps you can take to ensure that the items you write and the procedures you use to administer and grade the exam are fair and defensible.

Throughout this book, the suggestions put forth on how to go about the art and science of creating and scoring exams will all find their roots in one or more of the three important factors of test quality: validity, reliability, and fairness.

CHAPTER 3:

Deciding on the Test Format

Most likely, you have already made the decision of what type of test you will be creating. After all, the size of your class matters. In classes with a large number of students, multiple choice questions tend to be the most frequently used question format (Parkes, Fix & Harris, 2003; Pigge & Marso, 1988). Even so, it is good to understand the research underlying the pros and cons of different formats.

This next section provides a summary of this research. How do different types of items compare to each other? Later, the chapter will cover how different types of items can impact validity, reliability and fairness. Finally, you will read about a framework for making decisions about how to score your test (scoring may seem straightforward enough, but you may be making decisions you are not aware of).

Common Types of Items

Many different types of items have been created through the years and new item formats are being developed all the time as technologies continue to advance. However, there are classic item types that have been used for decades and will most likely continue to be used for decades to come. These are listed in Table 3-1.

Table 3-1. Common Types of Items

Category	Item Type
Selected Response	Multiple choice
	True/false
	Matching
Constructed Response	Open-ended
	(short answer, completion, or fill-in-the-blank)
	Essay

Selected response items present choices for the examinee, whereas constructed response items require that the examinee produce an answer.

Yes, there are many, many more types of items in the world, such as performance assessment items (for example, lab procedures and interviews). Table 3-1 just lists common types that will be covered in this book. The following are some quick examples of each type.

Examples

Multiple Choice

Circle the letter next to the best answer.

Which element is the lightest?

A. Hydrogen
B. Helium
C. Oxygen
D. Nitrogen

Correct answer: A

True/False

Next to each statement, circle T if the statement is true or F if the statement is false.

T F   Helium is the lightest element.

Correct answer: F

Matching

> There are two columns. Column A lists descriptions of elements. Column B lists elements. On the line next to each description, write the letter from Column B that best matches the description. A letter may be selected once, multiple times, or not at all.

Column A		Column B
1. This is the lightest element.	___	A. Hydrogen
2. Air consists of mostly this element.	___	B. Helium
3. This element is considered a noble gas.	___	C. Oxygen
4. This element has one electron.	___	D. Nitrogen

> Correct answers: A, D, B, A

Open-ended

> Write a word or short phrase to answer the question.
>
> Which element is the lightest? _____
>
> Correct answer: Hydrogen

Essay

In the space provided, discuss the origin of the name hydrogen. Include contributions by both Cavendish and Lavoisier. Your essay will be graded on main ideas (10 points), supporting details (10 points), and writing mechanics (5 points).

Possible answer:

Hydrogen is the first element listed in the periodic table, but it did not always have this name. In 1767, Henry Cavendish described hydrogen as "inflammable air." Cavendish most likely chose this name because hydrogen is a colorless gas that is highly flammable. Cavendish published experiments showing that when inflammable air was exposed to a spark in the presence of oxygen, water formed. Based on this discovery, Antoine Lavoisier coined the term hydrogène in 1787. The name was created by combining the Greek stem hydr- meaning "water" and the Greek ending –gen meaning "producing," which together means "water producing." The name hydrogen persisted and continues to describe the most abundant element observed in the universe.

Comparison of Item Types

There are different criteria for choosing the best types of items for your test. For example, ease and speed of grading could be the most important factor for some instructors; while other instructors might consider which item types best elicit higher-level thinking.

Guessing is also an issue to consider. For multiple choice, true/false, and matching questions, the answer is always provided, which invites a certain degree of guessing. In contrast, for open-ended items and essays, students have to generate their own answers, which reduces incidents of guessing but can make the item more difficult to grade. (Decisions need to be made regarding how to handle incomplete answers and spelling errors, for example. The topic of scoring is addressed in more detail in Chapters 5 and 9.)

Table 3-2 presents a comparison of different item types.

Table 3-2. Comparison of Item Types

Item Type	Speed of Grading	Higher-level Thinking	Guessing
Multiple Choice	faster	if well-crafted	yes
True/False	faster	less likely	yes
Matching	faster	if well-crafted	yes
Open-Ended	medium	if well-crafted	no
Essay	slower	yes	no

Different sections of your test might employ a variety of item types to balance some of the advantages and disadvantages across formats. There is also research that can help inform your decisions.

Research on Item Types

When researchers compare item types, they evaluate different metrics. Usually, they analyze a subset of the following measures: item difficulty, item discrimination, test reliability, and test validity. Again, item difficulty is how easy or difficult an item is; item discrimination is an item's ability to detect a high-performing student from a low-performing student; test reliability is how consistent a test is; and test validity is the degree to which a test is measuring what it is intended to measure in support of score interpretation.

Multiple Choice

By far, the item type that has enjoyed the most attention in the literature is multiple choice. And often, research on other item types is couched in terms of how the item type measures up to the canonical multiple choice question. According to this research, multiple choice, when done right, is robust and reliable and is one of the best choices, at least with regard to selected-response items (Bennett, Ward, Rock, & LaHart, 1990; Frisbie, 1974; Oosterhof & Glasnapp, 1974; Hancock, Thiede, Sax & Michael, 1993).

True/False

Unfortunately, empirical research has not supported the use of true/false items. For one, research studies have shown that true/false items are not able to discriminate well compared to multiple choice items (Frisbie, 1973; Harris & Changas, 1994; Oosterhof & Glasnapp, 1974). Moreover, in several studies, researchers have found that the reliability of tests with true/false items was significantly worse than tests with multiple choice items (Harris & Changas, 1994; Hancock, Thiede, Sax, & Michael, 1993).

If that weren't enough, other issues plague true/false items as well. For example, Cronbach (1942) reported that empirically, true items are not as valid and reliable as false items. This disparity within the same item type raises suspicions about what true/false items are actually measuring and whether or not they are unidimensional. Are true items measuring the same trait as false items? Some instructors might be tempted to add more false items to their test for reliability reasons, but it is unclear whether or not a larger proportion of false items might invite a response bias, since we know that students can detect frequency patterns in answer keys and exploit this information when guessing (Evans, 1984).

Guessing, in general, is another concern. Given that there are only two possible choices (true or false), the probability of guessing and getting an item correct is 0.50. This is a high probability. Test publishers are always trying to reduce the amount of guessing on tests so that genuine content mastery can be assessed. It is no surprise that true/false items do not appear in large-scale high-stakes tests (Haladyna & Rodriguez, 2013).

Further, evidence exists that true/false items tend to measure lower-level cognitive functioning compared to standard multiple choice items (Downing, Baranowski, Grosso, & Norcini, 1995). Educators often emphasize moving away from assessing lower-level fact knowledge, in favor of assessing higher-level thinking such as analyzing, applying, and evaluating (Haladyna & Rodriguez, 2013). Although not impossible, the prospects of probing these higher levels with true/false items are much less promising.

Together, these findings do not bode well for the true/false item type. In fact, others have acknowledged these disadvantages and have invented alternatives. For example, some instructors ask students to modify the false statements to make them true (Kubiszyn & Borich, 2003). However, if efficient item writing is a motivating factor for using true/false items, then the research findings suggest that instead, it would be better to create multiple choice items with two alternatives (A or B).

Matching

Matching items tend to be excluded from large-scale standardized tests; however, an exception to this is in the medical domain where matching items have enjoyed a long history in licensing exams.

Although some have claimed that matching items usually consist of extremely specific content and therefore might be considered too limiting (Haladyna & Rodriguez, 2013), the medical field has shown that matching items can extend into higher-order thinking. For example, some items are constructed such that they describe scenarios of patients with different symptoms. Each patient scenario is then matched with a diagnosis. Researchers have found that these item types perform quite well (Case & Swanson, 1998). In medical assessments, the traditional matching item type has only recently been replaced by an extended matching format in which a longer vignette is included at the beginning of the item (Case & Swanson, 1993). In one research study, a higher reliability was observed for a test with extended matching items compared to a traditional multiple choice test (Fenderson, Damjanov, Robeson, Veloski, & Rubin, 1997).

So, evidence shows that the matching item type has considerable potential when done right.

A Little History on the Origin of Item Types

Many different item types have been created, labeled, and trialed in the medical field. In 1953, the National Board of Medical Examiners (NBME) started to include standard multiple choice items in its medical licensing exams after extensive research with the Educational Testing Service. Previous to this, the tests consisted of written essays. Since this time, the NBME has assigned arbitrary letter labels to test item types simply based on when they were first originated. Thus, the standard, single-answer multiple choice item is described as an A-Type item.

Open-Ended

Open-ended items require a student to write down a single word or short phrase as a response. Similar item types include fill-in-the-blank, completion, and any other item that requires a student to construct a short response. Open-ended items appear frequently in tests, and for good reason. The appeal of these items is that they require students to recall and not just recognize information. In contrast, multiple choice items always present the correct answer as a choice, and for this reason, multiple choice items tend to be easier than items that require a constructed response[1] (Heim & Watts, 1967).

Further, open-ended items function very well on tests, and have even better psychometric properties than multiple choice items. Ward (1982) found that reliability was higher for tests with open-ended items compared to tests with multiple choice items. Oosterhof and Coats (1984) compared different item formats in a test of business finance. Two of these item formats were open-ended items and standard multiple choice items. They found that open-ended items were significantly more difficult than multiple choice items and were more reliable.

Open-ended items have also been shown to be better than multiple choice items for diagnostic purposes (Birenbaum & Tatuoka, 1987), and they result in better retention (McDaniel, Roediger, & McDermott, 2007).

The main reason items of this type do not appear more universally is that they must be hand-graded on paper-and-pencil tests. The other drawback is that since the wording of these items needs to be very specific to avoid ambiguity, they are often not written to assess higher-level cognitive processing (Kubiszyn & Borich, 2010).

---

[1] However, when the content is arithmetic or mathematical reasoning, the two test formats appear to have the same level of difficulty (Frederiksen & Satter, 1953; Traub & Fisher, 1977).

Essays

The main advantage of essay questions is that they give students the opportunity to exercise higher-level cognitive processing including synthesizing information, formulating arguments, and displaying creativity.

However, some researchers have challenged the notion that essays are better than multiple choice tests. For example, Bridgeman and Lewis (1994) found that the correlations between freshman course grades and multiple choice scores on AP exams were equivalent to correlations between grades and AP essay scores. The implication is that multiple choice exams, which are much easier to score, may be enough to measure content mastery. Other studies of AP tests also showed that essays did not contribute much more information than what was already provided by a multiple choice section (Wainer & Thissen, 1993; Walstad & Becker, 1994).

On the other hand, other studies have shown that there is a difference between the dimensions of knowledge probed by essays versus multiple choice (Becker & Johnston, 1999; Dufresne, 2002). Certainly, students perceive multiple choice tests as assessing lower-level thinking and essays as assessing higher-level thinking (Scouller, 1998). Essays also have the added benefit of better utilizing the practical skill of writing, which is essential to many professional careers.

The main drawback of essays is the amount of time it takes to grade them. Another problem is that the grading of essays is notoriously unreliable. In a recent study of teacher essay grading, Brimi (2011) asked 73 English teachers to score a single essay on a 100-point scale. All the teachers were professionally trained to use a specific grading system. The results showed vast variability in scores for the same essay, with a range between 50 to 96. Other research studies have also shown that essay-type items have a significantly lower reliability than multiple choice items (Bennett, Ward, Rock, & LaHart, 1990; Breland, 1987). Some tips on how to score essays reliably are presented in Chapter 9.

The following is a summary of findings from the research on item types:

(1) If you are choosing selected-response items, use multiple choice or matching items that target higher-level thinking. Avoid true/false items; they have lower discriminability and reliability than multiple choice items.

(2) If you are considering multiple choice versus open-ended items, select open-ended (if you have the time to invest in grading and if you can write open-ended items that target higher-level thinking).

(3) In the comparison of multiple choice items versus essays, the research is divided. Some argue that multiple choice items are better because they provide the same amount of

information and are more efficient to grade; others claim that essays assess deeper thinking such as the ability to construct an argument. So whichever you choose, there is some research supporting your decision.

Now, we bring the discussion to different types of items and how they relate to validity, reliability, and fairness.

Item Types and Validity

Most types of items that you may be considering have been used for decades in achievement tests (e.g., state achievement tests, advanced placement tests, and graduate subject tests). It would be unlikely for someone to challenge you about your choice of item types since there is an overwhelming amount of evidence that suggests that the common types can measure achievement. That said, think critically about whether or not your content domain requires something more. Would a written paper better prepare your students for the type of work expected in a career in the field? If you are teaching a lab, would a performance assessment be more appropriate? Granted, other assessment approaches may simply not be practical given the size of your class. But if you think through different options and document the reasoning behind your decisions, then you will further refine the definition of what you are intending to measure.

Item Types and Reliability

Another topic to consider when choosing item types is reliability. Recall that reliability can be improved with more items. Students, in most cases, could probably complete many more multiple choice items than short essays. However, when making decisions regarding which item types are most appropriate, validity reasons should trump reliability. When you do make your final decisions, think about how much information you will be gleaning from each item in your test and whether or not your measurement from the test will be precise enough for you to stand behind assigned grades. You will come up with a specific number of items for your test in the next chapter. For now, just consider issues such as whether or not your short essay test should be augmented with a multiple choice section to bolster your item count.

Another issue that arises when considering reliability is consistent scoring. If the test includes essays, open-ended questions, or performance assessments, thought needs to be devoted to how consistency will be maintained throughout the scoring process. (Some tips are provided in Chapter 9.)

Item Types and Fairness

When selecting types of items for your test, consider how different aspects of the tasks might introduce potential barriers for subgroups within your classroom population. For example, do some tasks impose time limits? Are there non-native speakers or students with learning disabilities in your class who might be affected by these time limits? If yes, then think carefully about why time limits are in place, if they are necessary, and how they might be modified.

Another topic to consider when thinking about fairness is the use of computerized equipment or other technology. Will all students have access to the same kind of equipment? If some students are able to use fast machines, while others have access only to slower equipment, then this difference might influence test scores. Also, it may be the case that some students will have experience with software required for an exam, but others may not and may need tutorials and extra support. For a fair testing administration, all examinees should have an equal opportunity to spin up on software well before the exam takes place.

Letter Grade Mapping

Letter grade mapping is the process of taking a numeric score (such as 90% correct) and associating it with a letter grade (for example, A-). This topic will be addressed in detail in Chapter 9, but it is a good idea to start thinking about it early in the test-development process.

Scoring Based on a Criterion

The majority of tests administered in university and college classes are aimed at determining how well students have mastered (and can apply) the material covered in class (Parkes, Fix & Harris, 2003). This goal lends itself to a criterion-referenced style of scoring. This means that the test scores are referenced against a *criterion* or a set standard of performance; namely, a list of things that the student should be able to do in order to pass your class (Kubiszyn & Borich, 2010). As an instructor or assistant to an instructor, you determine what the student needs to demonstrate in order to receive an A, B, C, D, or F. Therefore, according to this approach, if all students do everything that you require of them to receive an A, then every single student in your class should be given an A. Likewise, every student could get a C. Are you okay with this? Is your department okay with this? Some are and some are not.

With a criterion-referenced approach to scoring, the challenge is to determine what the student should demonstrate for each assigned grade. This criterion is important to consider as you are planning your test and writing your exam questions.

Scoring Based on the Group (Norm-Referenced)

As an alternative to criterion-referenced scoring, another approach is to adjust grades based on the group you have in your class. By most definitions, this means that average students will receive Cs; the highest performing students will receive As; and the lowest performing students will receive Fs. This style of scoring is called *grading on a curve*. The idea is that when we measure most things related to humans, the distribution forms a bell-shaped curve. With a bell-shaped curve, most people are in the middle range, and only a few are at the very high and low ends of the scale.

This style of assigning grades is related to norm-referenced scoring. For large standardized tests, much research is invested in sampling a representative group of test takers who will comprise the norming group, and scores from this norming group determine what the average grade should be. In the classroom setting, the norming group is usually the group of students in your class (or the group from the previous year's class). Your sample of students serves as a local norm that is used to adjust (or scale) the scores. This is a common practice among instructors when scoring essays; many instructors take the approach of reading through all the essays, ordering them from best to worst, and then assigning grades accordingly. With this approach, there will always be a spread of grades across students, but it is harder to articulate to an individual student why his or her paper was assigned a C and not a B-.

When grading on a curve, the challenge is to figure out where the cut points for each grade should be. Some recommendations of how to do this are presented in Chapter 9.

Regardless of whether you choose to take the criterion-referenced approach, the group-referenced approach, or an approach somewhere in the middle, understanding the differences and recognizing the reasons for your choices can help with your discussions with students regarding your expectations and grading style.

CHAPTER 4:

Creating a Test Blueprint

Before diving into the guidelines for each type of item, a common recommendation is to plan out the test at a high level first (Kubiszyn & Borich, 2010). An effective way to do this is to design a test blueprint.

What Will the Test Measure?

For the blueprint, one suggestion is first to define what you intend to measure (AERA, APA & NCME, 2014; DeVellis, 2012). What is the characteristic, trait, or construct that you are interested in evaluating? If you create a formal description of what it is you are hoping to measure, then you will have something concrete to reference when considering evidence of the test's construct validity.

Establishing Intended Uses and Interpretations

"The construct or constructs that the test is intended to assess should be described clearly."

- AERA, APA, & NCME, 2014
Standard 1.1

For most tests in academic settings, the construct will be achievement in a specific content area, such as *achievement in introductory biology.* More descriptive definitions can help you distinguish the current test from other tests you might administer throughout the year.

The following is an example of defining a test's construct:

> "The purpose of the test is to determine to what degree students enrolled in Course 201, *Intro to Neuropsychology,* understand frequently occurring neuropsychological diseases, their psychological symptoms, and biological underpinnings. High scores on the test are intended to be interpreted as mastery of these concepts, while low scores indicate a level of achievement below mastery. Test scores will contribute 20% toward the final class grade."

In the above example, the construct is mastery in understanding the listed content, and the target examinees are students in the class. The purpose of the test is to measure understanding and mastery of the concepts in order to help assign a final grade.

Listing Content

The next step toward creating a test blueprint is to list out the content to be covered on the test. By documenting the alignment between the test content and the content covered in your course, not only will you help yourself in the creation of the test, but you will be providing supporting evidence of the test's content validity that can later be referenced if students challenge the test.

In fact, you will be doing what large test publishers do when they want to show evidence of content validity. Granted test publishers usually go through some extra steps of hiring experts to review this documentation, but the principle is the same: it is simply a logical exercise showing that the test is accurately reflecting the right material.

Design and Development of Educational Assessments

"When a test is used as an indicator of achievement in an instructional domain ... evidence of the extent to which the test samples the range of knowledge and elicits the processes reflected in the target domain should be provided."

- AERA, APA, & NCME, 2014
Standard 12.4

The test blueprint will give you a logical structure that defines the importance of each topic covered on the test in a simple way and maps this information to the items on your test.

Just as a side note, some formal textbooks on educational measurement (Kubiszyn & Borich, 2010) recommend a three-stage approach to classroom measurement in which instructors write educational objectives (Stage 1), activities aimed at teaching these objectives (Stage 2), and then test questions aligned with the objectives (Stage 3).

Including a Variety of Difficulty Levels and Thought Levels

In order for test scores to be mapped to grades, test scores must be able to distinguish different levels of performance. It does the instructor no good to present all simple questions on a test. The questions will be too easy and test scores from such a test will not be able to discriminate a student who understands key concepts in the class from a student who does not. Likewise, a test with all difficult items is not useful either. The goal is to include questions with a range of difficulties.

Additionally, many sources recommend including questions that cover a range of levels of thought (Kubiszyn & Borich, 2010). For example, some questions might probe knowledge of facts, whereas others might require higher-level thinking such as evaluating a process or perspective. Research has shown that most tests are skewed toward containing too many items at the lower levels of thinking (Fleming & Chambers, 1983; Frederiksen, Mislevey & Bejar, 2012). In fact, Pigge and Marso (1988) found that of 175 actual teacher-written tests, a whopping 72% of the items were measuring ability at the lowest knowledge level.

To ameliorate this problem of too many items focusing on rote knowledge, many educators recommend that test creators make a conscious effort to write items that span a range of levels (Haladyna & Rodriguez, 2013; Kubiszyn & Borich, 2010). A common way to do this is to use Bloom's Taxonomy (or a simplified version of the taxonomy). According to Bloom (1956), there are six levels of reasoning, and each requires a different level of abstraction in educational settings. The six levels are Knowledge, Comprehension, Analysis, Application, Synthesis, and Evaluation. Later, Bloom, Englehart, Hill, Furst, and Krathwohl (1984) revised the taxonomy (also known as the Taxonomy of Educational Objectives for the Cognitive Domain) by describing the levels in terms of cognitive complexity and by rearranging the order of two of the levels (Application and Analysis). Then it was later revised such that Synthesis was changed to Create and placed at the highest cognitive level (Anderson et al., 2001).

Table 4-1. Different Phases of Bloom's Taxonomy

Classic Bloom's Taxonomy	1984 Version	2001 Version
Knowledge	Knowledge	Knowledge
Comprehension	Comprehension	Comprehension
Analysis	Application	Application
Application	Analysis	Analysis
Synthesis	Synthesis	Evaluation
Evaluation	Evaluation	Create

Although many educators recommend using Bloom's Taxonomy to help guide the level of thinking required for test questions, research on the topic has not corroborated the existence of six distinct levels (for a review, see Haladyna & Rodriguez, 2013). The reason for this may be that students use different cognitive processes to answer the same question. For example, it is known that subject-matter experts are able to pull complex information from memory due to their years of experience and well-developed mastery of a content area, whereas novices must rely on other, less efficient cognitive mechanisms to tackle complex problems (Anderson, 1990). Additionally a student's ability to use test-taking strategies to figure out answers can confound attempts to classify the cognitive level of items (Solano-Flores & Li, 2009).

Some have simplified the taxonomy by collapsing the six levels into three. Different researchers have done this in different ways. As one example, Crooks (1988) used the categories Knowledge, Comprehension / Application, and Problem Solving (where Application is when information is transferred to a new situation).

So, the bottom line for someone creating a test is that it is probably a good idea to keep Bloom's Taxonomy in mind, but realistically, test questions that target two or three levels of abstraction should suffice. What is certain is that a test should include questions that go beyond simple knowledge of facts.

Test Blueprint Example

Together, the information about what content will be covered, the difficulty level of items, and the cognitive complexity of items can be represented in a tabular format called a test blueprint (also referred to as a test specification, table of specifications, or two-way grid).

With regard to difficulty, an assumption can be made that items aimed at eliciting higher-level thinking will be more difficult. Although this might not always be the case, it helps simplify the test blueprint. Predicting an item's difficulty can be challenging, so the notions of item difficulty and cognitive complexity are combined for the purposes of item writing.

Figure 4-2 shows what a test blueprint might look like. The test blueprint guides decisions regarding the number of questions for different content topics and abstraction levels and overall grade proportions of the different sections of the test.

Test Blueprint for Exam 1, *Intro to Psychology*, Course 125

Intended Use of Test: The purpose of Exam 1 is to determine to what degree students understand basic concepts in the field of psychology covered in the first five weeks of class including neurobiology, human psychological development, and sensation and perception.

Examinees: The examinees will be 145 students enrolled in the Fall Course 125, *Introduction to Psychology.*

Test Duration: The test is intended to be taken during the standard 50-minute class period scheduled on October 23.

Scoring: There will be 100 points possible on the test. Responses to multiple choice items will be marked on a machine-readable form and will be worth 2 points each. Responses to open-ended questions will be written directly on the test and will be worth 4 points each. Scoring open-ended questions will allow for partial credit, such that responses that are correct but misspelled, grammatically incorrect, partially incomplete or ambiguous will be awarded 2 points. Open-ended questions are given more weight because they require constructing responses as opposed to recognizing information.

High scores on the test are intended to be interpreted as mastery of concepts basic to psychology, while low scores indicate a level of achievement below mastery.

Topics	Importance of Topic	Percentage of Section	Total # of Items	Cognitive Level		
				Low	Mid	High
Section 1: Multiple Choice (2 points/item)						
Topic A	Mid	20%	7	3	2	2
Topic B	Low	10%	3	1	1	1
Topic C	High	30%	10	3	4	3
Topic D	Mid	20%	7	2	3	2
Topic E	Mid	20%	7	2	2	3
SUB-TOTAL		100%	34	11	12	11
34 items at 2 points/item = 68 points						
Section 2: Open-Ended Questions (4 points/item)						
Topic C	High	50%	4	1	1	2
Topic D	Mid	25%	2	1	1	
Topic E	Mid	25%	2		1	1
SUB-TOTAL		100%	8	2	3	3
8 items at 4 points/item = 32 points						
TOTAL			42	13	15	14
68 points + 32 points = 100 points						

Figure 4-2. Example of a Test Blueprint.

Not only can a test blueprint ensure that all relevant content areas are covered on the test, but it also provides information regarding the number of items, which is closely linked to the test's reliability. The key is to include enough items so that there is sufficient information to make an accurate interpretation of a student's mastery of the content covered in your class. Generally, I find that tests that have at least 40 items have acceptable reliability. Of course, time constraints and fatigue also need to be considered. A general guideline is to allow at least 30 seconds per question (for multiple choice items) (Srinivasa & Adkoli, 1989; Lowman, 1984).

If you have no idea whether or not the reliability will be good enough, just allow for as many items as is reasonable in the given time frame. Then after the test, calculate reliability (see Appendix A) and use this information to plan your next test. Over time, you will gather enough information to be able to predict what the reliability will be.

Additionally, a common practice in test development is to create more items than you need for a test so that you can vet items. For standardized tests, test developers often create six times as many items as those used on the actual exam. You are not creating a standardized test, so you can scale back this number and possibly create 10% to 20% more than you need to allow for some item vetting. The vetting will take place as you select the final items. Also, including some additional items in the final test will allow you to discard a few low-functioning items after the test has been taken.

Reviewing the Test Blueprint

After creating a test blueprint, you might consider having someone else, such as another instructor, review it. By having another set of eyes look over your blueprint before you write specific items, you may save yourself significant time if your reviewer identifies a legitimate problem such as underrepresentation of a subtopic, unrealistic time expectations or even equipment problems that might impede automatic scoring.

Regardless of whether you or another expert is reviewing your test blueprint, make sure you consider the test blueprint in the context of validity. Does the test blueprint accurately depict the important content areas that you have been emphasizing in the course? Could a student potentially complain that the content areas on the test did not align with the course? If you can confidently answer these questions and support these answers with evidence, then you are well on your way toward creating a quality test.

Once you have a final test blueprint, it is time to dive into creating the content of the test. Let's start writing items!

CHAPTER 5:

Writing Items

It takes time and skill to create items that are original, unambiguous and effective. For me, the item writing process begins by consulting the test blueprint to see which topics I want to cover. Then, I ask myself some questions: What do I want my students to know about this topic? How do I want them to be able to use this knowledge? How can they demonstrate their mastery? These questions get the creative juices flowing, but more importantly, they link back to the goals and objectives of the course. Never lose sight of your purpose. Your goal is to instill in your students the knowledge and skills important to the content area of the course.

Then, after much thinking, I write a draft of an item, often with scribbling and multiple revisions. Finally, I review the guidelines in this chapter. More often than not, I have violated a guideline, and so I attempt to fix the item accordingly. The bulk of this chapter is dedicated to describing these guidelines including the basis for them and the reasons why they are worth following.

Why Should You Care About Item Writing Guidelines?

Luckily, we have the benefit of learning from a large body of research on what makes for good and bad items. Before diving into specific guidelines, though, it is important to address why these guidelines are worth following. In all cases, the recommendations presented here are based on empirical research. The research generally goes like this: somebody somewhere did a study manipulating something about an item and found that there was a negative impact – therefore, you should avoid doing this type of thing in your own items. Now, unlike academic articles, the discussions in this book related to guidelines do not present an exhaustive review of all experiments published in all journals. And, indeed, in many cases, there are debates about guidelines in the literature because some researchers find an effect, while others report null results. The perspective here is that even when some null results appear in the literature, I include the guideline anyway, especially when researchers are observing a noticeable change in item performance that should not be ignored.

When researchers conduct experiments on items, they usually focus on how changes to items affect a set number of measures: item difficulty, item discrimination, test reliability, and test validity. Most often, researchers look at how changes to an item influence the item's difficulty. Changes that give test takers clues as to the right answer (apart from the content of the item) and make the item easier are considered bad. Also changes that make an item more difficult because of confusion or some other factor that is not directly related to what is being assessed are considered bad. However, be aware that increasing difficulty is not *always* a bad thing. As long as the change is consistent with the construct that is being measured, then increasing item difficulty might be fine and might extend the range of items in your test.

Another factor that researchers often consider is how a change to an item affects the item's ability to discriminate high-performing students from low-performing students. Generally, lowering item discrimination is considered a bad thing.

Even more important are how changes affect reliability and validity. Unfortunately, these variables are not analyzed as frequently in the literature, but when they do appear, they have considerable impact. Changes to items that decrease reliability or that decrease validity are definitely bad and these types of patterns should be avoided in your item writing.

So, why pay attention to guidelines at all? The reason is to avoid doing something that has been shown empirically to degrade the quality of a test by introducing construct-irrelevant variance or by reducing the test's reliability, validity, or ability to discriminate. Unfortunately, most of the guidelines take the form of "Don't do this," and "Don't do that." So, brace yourself. At the end of the chapter is a checklist so that you can easily remind yourself of the guidelines without having to trudge through all the details.

First, here are a few pointers that apply to all item types.

General Guidelines for All Item Types

Create Original Content

Many item writers are in a pinch to get an exam out, and they tend to borrow a bit too heavily from the wording and examples in the text. In fact, I knew a professor who did this and not surprisingly, many of his students complained that he had given them a memory test and not a test accurately representing the content of the course. For the students, the test lacked validity. The best way to avoid this situation is to avoid direct wording from textbooks and create original items that rely on important concepts from your course. This recommendation is supported by research (Kaplan & Saccuzzo, 2013). So do what you can to resist the temptation.

Research Supports Items That Are Independent of One Another

Research suggests that items should be independent of one another (Kaplan & Saccuzzo, 2013). This means that the student should not have to correctly answer Question 1 in order to answer Question 2. This scenario often occurs when there is a two-step process, or when choices are exhausted in a matching item. Also, test theorists posit that all items on a test should be independent (e.g., Lord, 1952). For these reasons, it is recommended that items avoid dependencies on one another.

Keep the Language Simple

The language used in an item can have an impact on the item's functioning. Consistent with intuition, if an item has difficult vocabulary and complex sentence structure, then the item will be more difficult to answer (Cassels & Johnstone, 1984). For example, an item that uses the phrase, "a liquid other than water," is easier compared to an item with the phrase, "non-aqueous solvent." The implications of this are complex. On the one hand, appropriate vocabulary might be something that shows mastery of a content area. On the other, excessively difficult language can introduce construct-irrelevant variance. If a non-native speaker of English takes the test, and this person's score suffers not because of knowledge of the content but because of differences in language ability, then the test might be considered unfair. The concept applies not only to the words used in the item, but also the sentence structure. Cassels and Johnstone (1984) also found that items with short, simple sentences were easier compared to items with identical content but more complex sentence structure (for example, embedded clauses). If you are not teaching a language class, then scores biased against non-native speakers might indicate that the test is also measuring the construct of language in addition to your content area.

The issue of appropriate language is not to be taken lightly. The topic is raised explicitly in the *Standards* (AERA, APA, & NCME, 2014), where it states, "Test developers should use language in tests that is consistent with the purposes of the tests and that is familiar to as wide a range of test takers as possible." Additionally, court rulings have brought to light potential violations of civil rights because of the language used on tests (Diana v. State Board of Education).

So, the bottom line is, authoritative organizations recommend that the language you use in your items should not be excessively unfamiliar to your students unless such language is consistent with your goal of testing the content domain, for example, when certain terms are important to know for operating successfully in a specific field. Otherwise, for the sake of fairness, keep it simple.

Research Supports Succinct Items

Related to this is the idea of keeping the item succinct and free from extraneous material. Sometimes, item writers introduce additional information to an item in order to create a distraction from the relevant material, possibly to make an item harder. And, in fact, it has been observed that lengthy items result in increased item difficulty (Cassels & Johnstone, 1984; Rimland, 1960(a); Schmeiser & Whitney, 1973). However, as a principle, making an item harder in and of itself is not devastating. When the item writing starts decreasing discriminabiliy, reliability, or validity, then there is definitely cause to worry. Unfortunately for those verbose item writers out there, research has shown that when items contain irrelevant information, item discrimination, reliability, and validity decrease, too (Rimland, 1960(a); Schmeiser & Whitney, 1973; Schmeiser & Whitney, 1975; Schrock & Mueller, 1982). Therefore, a common suggestion is to keep the wording of an item pithy.

Avoid Certain Words Such as "Usually" that Add Ambiguity

The vagueness of some words such as "often" and "usually" presents ambiguity that can hamper the functioning of an item (Kaplan & Saccuzzo, 2013). For example, researchers found that there was considerable overlap on how a group of 60 item writers interpreted the terms "frequently" and "rarely" (Case & Swanson, 1998). Such ambiguity hiders the functioning of the item. An alternative is to use absolute numbers, for example, "between 40% and 60% of ..."

Guidelines for Specific Item Types

What follows are guidelines relevant for specific item types. The multiple choice section is definitely the longest because it has enjoyed the most attention in the literature.

Guidelines for Multiple Choice Items

Multiple choice items are the most popular kind of test item used by instructors (Parkes, Fix & Harris, 2003). Surveys have shown that most students prefer multiple choice questions over essays (Struyven, Dochy, & Janssens, 2005). Moreover, the multiple choice format has also been thoroughly researched and therefore can be easily supported in the face of challenges (Downing & Haladyna, 2004).

Format of a Multiple Choice Item

We are all quite familiar with what a conventional multiple choice item looks like. But let's go over the structure to align ourselves regarding the terms used to describe its anatomy. All multiple choice items consist of a *stem*, which is the main part of the question or statement, followed by a list of *choices* or alternatives labeled A, B, C, D, etc. For most multiple choice items, one of these choices is the correct answer and the rest of the choices are *distractors*. The stem appears first and the choices are listed, one per line in a logical order.

The following is an example of the format of a multiple choice item.

Directions: Circle the letter next to the best answer.

A good multiple choice item has which of the following?

A. A stem that quotes the textbook
B. One correct answer
C. One distractor
D. A distractor that high-performing students will select

Correct answer: B

First, I will discuss issues related to stems, followed by issues related to choices.

Issues Related to Stems

Research Supports the Use of Complete Sentences/Questions in the Stem

Some researchers suggest that the stem should be a complete sentence or question as opposed to a fragment (Kaplan & Saccuzzo, 2013). For example, the item above should read, "A good multiple choice item has which of the following?" as opposed to "A good multiple choice item has …" The reason for this is that researchers have found that multiple choice items using fragments instead of complete sentences often have unnecessarily lower correct response rates (Dudycha & Carpenter, 1973;

Eisley, 1990; Kent, Jones, & Schmeiser, 1974; Schmeiser & Whitney, 1973; Schmeiser & Whitney, 1975). Given this consistent finding, it is recommended that stems be complete sentences or questions as opposed to fragments.

Consensus about Negative Wording

Negative wording can be a popular technique, for example, "Which of the following is NOT true?" or "All of the following are true EXCEPT ..." Many researchers suggest that this style of item should be used with caution. The reason is that the negative wording can create unnecessary complexity and cognitive load that goes beyond the scope of the item's content. Both Cassels and Johnstone (1984) and Dudycha and Carpenter (1973), for example, systematically compared negatively and positively worded items and did indeed show that negative items were more difficult. Tamir (1993) also reported higher difficulty for items that were written at a high cognitive level and that had negative wording. In fact, in a review of textbooks that discuss how to write multiple choice items, 31 out of 35 authors recommended that this type of item be avoided (Haladyna & Downing, 1989). In a different review of 20 textbooks about item writing, over half recommended avoiding negative wording (Kaplan & Saccuzzo, 2013). The National Board of Medical Examiners also recommends avoiding negative reasoning in items (Case & Swanson, 1993).

If an item with negative wording is used, researchers recommend that the negative word be typographically highlighted by using boldface or capitals (or both) to ensure that students are aware that they will be flipping their logic to the negative perspective (Haladyna & Downing, 1989).

In related research, others have found that the direction of comparison can affect the difficulty of an item (Cassels & Johnstone, 1984). For example, having a chemistry student figure out the "most abundant" element in a mixture is easier than the "least abundant." Again, if using such a technique to manipulate difficulty, make sure to highlight the key word that signifies the way in which students should be thinking about the information.

Issues Related to Choices

One of the more difficult tasks of writing multiple choice items is to generate compelling distractors. Commonly, educators have recommended creating distractors by using students' common errors (King, Gardner, Zucker, Jorgensen, 2004; Minstrell, 2000). By all means, try this. If you find it difficult knowing what common student errors are, rest assured that you can create good distractors by imagining what they might be or by using other methods. Also, save yourself time by creating no more than three distractors.

Research Supports Three or Four Choices

You might have the impression that the more choices a multiple choice question has (up to about five), the better. However, research has shown that there is little difference between the effectiveness of items that have three, four, or five choices (Baghaei & Amrahi, 2011; Haladyna & Downing, 1989; Haladyna & Downing, 1993). In fact, if more choices are introduced, they have little impact on the functioning of the item because some of the distractors are infrequently or never selected. Rarely are all the distractors functioning well in teacher-written tests (Haladyna & Downing, 1993; Tarrant, Ware and Mohammed, 2009). Basically, it is as if these items do not have additional distractors at all because the distractors simply are not doing their job of distracting. Interestingly, the psychometric properties of items with only three choices (one answer and two distractors) are just as good as those items with five choices or more (Rodriguez, 2005). Therefore, the recommendation is to save time and write items with only three or four choices (Anastasi & Urbina, 1997).

In fact, some researchers (Lord, 1977; Rodriguez, 2005) suggest that the optimal number of choices in a multiple choice item is three. More distractors do not improve the functioning of the item; more distractors take time to write, especially the fourth and fifth distractors (Haladyna & Rodriguez, 2013); and more distractors also add to the time it takes students to take the test (which would be better spent answering more questions).

One caveat to this suggestion is that the fewer choices in a multiple choice item, the higher the probability of guessing the correct answer. Haladyna and Rodriguez (2013) argue that moving from a 25% chance of guessing to a 33% chance of guessing is small and can be offset by creating a longer test (which will have better reliability).

Ultimately, the choice between two and three distractors is yours – what is clear, though, is that you can save yourself some time and not bother with four distractors (or more).

In a similar vein, if a distractor is not plausible, then students tend not to choose the distractor and it is as if the distractor is not even a part of the item. Sometimes this can occur if an item writer includes a silly distractor for comic relief. If you're a joker and love to interject your style into your tests, feel free by all means, but be aware that the distractor is not providing you with any additional information about your students. Research confirms that when items contain choices that are not plausible, the items are easier (Weiten, 1984).

Research Does Not Support Complex Choice Combinations

There is a certain type of multiple choice item in which the choices are combinations of choices, for example, "A and B," or "B and C but not D." This type of item was labeled the K-Type by the National Board of Medical Examiners. Research on this item type suggests that complex combinations should be avoided for several reasons. First, items with complex choice combinations are artificially more difficult (Case & Swanson, 1993; Hughes & Trimble, 1965; Mueller, 1975; Tripp & Tollefson, 1985; Weiten, 1982). Most likely, this is the case because of their undue complex logic.

Second, compared to standard multiple choice items, items with complex choice combinations are less effective in sharply discriminating high-performing students from low-performing students (Case & Swanson, 1993; Mueller, 1975; Rossi, McCrady & Paolino, 1978; Sireci, Wiley, & Keller, 1998; Weiten, 1982). One reason for this is that students who have partial knowledge and can identify one correct or incorrect choice will be able to eliminate choices based on logic as opposed to content knowledge.

Third, a study by Weiten (1982) found that tests that contained items with complex choice combinations had less internal reliability. Additionally, a study by Hughes and Trimble (1965) showed that items with complex choices were less valid. In their study, Hughes and Trimble found that the correlation between test scores from a constructed-response test and scores from a test with complex choice items were much worse than the correlation between the constructed-response test and a test with standard multiple choice questions. Since constructed-response items can provide better insight into a student's level of knowledge (full or partial), it is a good standard for a validity comparison. From this perspective, standard multiple choice items appear to be better measurement tools.

Finally, a research study by Huntley and Plake (1988) found that items with complex choice combinations required more cognitive processing and took longer for students to complete. This additional processing time required by the students leads to inefficiency.

Consistent with these findings, items with complex choice combinations have been removed from medical licensing exams because they are too complicated, do not discriminate well, and result in lower test reliability (Case & Swanson, 1993).

Research Does Not Support "All of the Above" Items

Although writing items that include a choice of "all of the above" is a common practice, research has suggested that this type of multiple choice item should be avoided. Here is why: the correct answer is so often "all of the above," that students have an increased probability of selecting the correct answer because of good test-taking abilities as opposed to knowledge of the material on the test. Students can select "all of the above" without even reading the question and have a high chance of getting the answer right (Mueller, 1975; Poundstone, 2014). Even if the answer is not "all of the above," the student can simply find one option that is not true to eliminate the choice of "all of the above." There is also some evidence that items with "all of the above" have a decreased ability to discriminate high-performing students from low-performing students (Mueller, 1975). In a review of 20 textbooks listing advice about item writing, avoiding "all of the above" was the most frequently mentioned piece of advice (Kaplan & Saccuzzo, 2013).

Research Does Not Support "None of the Above" Items

Likewise, another common practice is to write items that include "none of the above" as a choice. It is clear from research that a choice of "none of the above" makes an item more difficult (Boynton, 1950; Crehan & Haladyna, 1989; Forsyth & Spratt, 1980; Frary, 1991; Knowles & Welch, 1992; Mueller, 1975; Rimland, 1960(b); Tollefson, 1987; Wesman & Bennett, 1946; Williamson & Hopkins, 1967). Because some of these experiments were tightly controlled using the same questions with and without "none of the above" across tests, the increase in difficulty is specifically related to the existence of the choice of "none of the above," and not to the content of the item. Most likely some other factor aside from the content such as increased cognitive processing appears to be driving performance down.

Additionally, a more disconcerting finding, although not present in all studies, is that a choice of "none of the above" comparatively reduces the item's ability to discriminate (Dudycha & Carpenter, 1973; Forsyth & Spratt, 1980; Haladyna & Downing, 1989; Mueller, 1975; Wesman & Bennett, 1946). So, the ideal pattern of high-performing students getting the answer right and low-performing students getting the answer wrong is decreased; and decreasing discrimination raises a red flag for the validity of a test.

Further, overall test reliability has been shown to decrease with the use of "none of the above" items (Tollefson, 1987).

These patterns do not support the goal of creating a reliable and valid test, and that is why many researchers try to dissuade item writers from using "none of the above." Some researchers who have found little difference in discrimination between items with and without "none of the above" advise that "none of the above" can be used with caution (Frary, 1991; Osterlind, 1989). And it is certainly true that some "none of the above" items can have good psychometric properties. That said, in my opinion, there are far too many experiments that *do* show a decrease in discrimination and reliability to warrant its use.

If you are still undecided, here are some other points to consider. First, one of the most frequently mentioned advice from a review of 20 textbooks on item writing was to avoid "none of the above" (second only to the recommendation to avoid "all of the above") (Kaplan & Saccuzzo, 2013). Second, these items tend to take longer to complete (Wesman & Bennett, 1946); this is time that might be better spent on more questions (since more questions tend to increase the reliability of a test). Third, Gross (1994) makes a logical statement that a student could correctly answer "none of the above" and still not know the information asked in the question. (What is the capital of Texas?) He argues that any item that awards a correct answer to someone with misinformation should disqualify its use. Finally, a manual from the National Board of Medical Examiners dissuades item writers from using "none of the above" for the following reason:

> If the correct response is intended to be one of the other listed options, knowledgeable students can be faced with a dilemma because they have to decide between a very detailed perfect option and the one that you have intended as correct. They can often construct an option that is more correct than the one you intended to be correct. Use of "none of the above" essentially turns the item into a true/false item; each option has to be evaluated as more or less true than the universe of unlisted options.
>
> -Case and Swanson, 1993

Overall, the research shows that there are many reasons why not to use "none of the above," so the advice here is to avoid it.

Some Findings on What Makes Distractors More Difficult

Research has found that when students do not know an answer, they tend to be scared off by technical terms (Strang, 1977). For example, if an answer is unknown, a student will avoid choices that include words such as "isofilial" and "acropraxic" as opposed to choices that describe a concept with less jargon. There is no recommendation for or against using technical terms, it is just useful information for item writing.

We also know that when all the distractors are similar to the correct answer (for example, all the choices are tools in the same category), then, the item becomes more difficult than if some of the distractors are outside the category (Green, 1984).

Research Does Not Support Patterns that Benefit Testwiseness

Testwiseness describes the skill of doing well on tests, regardless of the content. Some students are simply better at deducing what was on the item writer's mind. Further, there are papers that explicitly highlight testwiseness strategies that exploit idiosyncrasies of the test constructor (Millman, Bishop, & Ebel, 1965; Sarnacki, 1979). So, even if the student does not have an innate ability to exploit cues in tests, the student can read these papers and learn how to do better on tests generally by detecting patterns (Sarnacki, 1979; Smith, 1982).

There are many patterns that appear in multiple choice items that give clues as to what the correct answer is regardless of the content of the item. Because these clues present an advantage to those students with good test-taking skills, they introduce construct-irrelevant variance to your test and should be avoided. Do tests at the college level really have clues in them? You bet they do – an analysis of real tests shows it (Brozo, Schmelzer & Spires, 1984). These clues are so prominent that researchers often makes pleas and suggestions in their articles:

> "Item writing training workshops should be made available to faculty…"

> -Brozo, Schmelzer & Spires, 1984

> "One approach to eliminating [testwise] TW effects suggests instructing test-makers in the principles of both test construction in general, and TW in particular."

> - Sarnacki, 1979

The following are specific examples of testwise clues to avoid in your items.

Choices That Are Related to One Another

Often item writers create items in which the choices vary with each other by only one or two elements, as in the following example:

Example of Related Choices Cue

Three factors related to test quality are the following:

A. Reliability, fairness, and bias
B. Reliability, validity, and ability
C. Reliability, validity, and fairness
D. Validity, fairness, and accuracy

Correct answer: C

If you were to look at these choices without thinking about the content, which answer would you choose? The fact that "reliability" is mentioned in three choices, "validity" is mentioned in three choices, and "fairness" is mentioned in three, gives you a clue. Some researchers have referred to this logical deduction as a Convergence strategy (Case & Swanson, 1993). Another variant of this issue is when the correct answer is among a pair of choices that are the opposite of one another.

This clue of related choices is listed first of all the other clues because it is so common. In a study of how often testwise clues occur in real exams, this one appeared most frequently (Brozo, Shmelzer, & Spires, 1984). Therefore, to avoid giving testwise students an advantage, researchers suggest avoiding choices that are the opposite of one another or that systematically vary (Kaplan & Saccuzzo, 2013).

Answers That Are the Longest Choice

Commonly in multiple choice items, the correct answer tends to be longer than associated distractors. In a study that looked at actual tests created by college and university instructors, when one choice was noticeably longer than the others, this choice was the correct answer 76% of time (Brozo, Schmelzer, & Spires, 1984). This cue was also the most frequent in a review of 100 actual seventh- and tenth-grade tests (Hughes, Salvia, & Bott, 1991).

Why is the longest choice so often the correct one? One reason is that item writers want to ensure that the correct choice is accurate, and therefore they add extra description to convey the truth precisely. In contrast, distractors may not require this extra verbiage. Students are privy to this pattern. Publishers of test taking strategies explicitly teach individuals about it (Poundstone, 2014; Sarnacki, 1979). And research has shown that when students are presented with unknown material, they more frequently select the longer answer compared to random guessing (Chase, 1964; Jones & Kaufman, 1975; Strang, 1977).

Unfortunately, when this cue appears in an item, the psychometric properties of the item suffer. Many studies have found that when an answer is noticeably longer than distractors, the item is significantly easier (Dunn & Goldstein, 1959; Evans, 1984; McMorris, Brown, Snyder, & Pruzek, 1972; Weiten, 1984). Also, Weiten (1984) observed that when choice length was a cue to the correct answer, an item was less able to discriminate.

Therefore, a common suggestion is to keep the choices similar in size.

Answers That Contain a Keyword

In some cases, the answer to a multiple choice item contains key vocabulary that is presented in the stem. The following is an example.

Example of a Keyword Cue

In the first half of the 20th century, which of the following groups discouraged immigration policies that could result in cheap *labor*?

A. *labor* unions
B. communists
C. business owners
D. farmers

Correct answer: A

Students notice this repetition of keywords and guess the correct answer more frequently. Several research studies have shown that when a keyword appears in both the stem and the answer, the item is easier overall (Carter, 1986; McMorris et al., 1972; Pyrczak, 1973; Weiten, 1984). Additionally, Weiten (1984) reported that when keywords from the stem are used in answer choices, item discrimination decreases.

When reviewing your items, then, search for keywords that are shared by both your stem and choices and rewrite items as necessary.

Answers That Are the Most General Choice

In an analysis of test questions written by college and university instructors, Brozo, Schmelzer, and Spires (1984) found that when one choice was noticeably more general than the others, the more general choice was the correct answer 81% of the time. The following is an example.

Example of a General Choice Cue

Which of the following best describes Shakespeare's history plays?

A. The histories are about English kings who reigned between 1000 and 1200 AD.
B. Shakespeare wrote the histories during the year he died.
C. They recount the lives of kings in the Tudor lineage.
D. They are about monarchs who reigned before Shakespeare's time.

Correct answer: D

In the example above, choices A, B, and C all provide specific details. Choice A gives a specific range of years that the kings reigned; choice B describes a specific year that the histories were written; and Choice C gives a specific hereditary line. In contrast, Choice D is more general because it uses the term "monarchs" as opposed to "kings" and refers to a large span of time ("before Shakespeare's time"). Because Choice D is noticeably more general, students are more apt to select it, even if they do not know about Shakespeare's histories.

To help avoid this pattern, identify the most general choice in each item and make sure it is not always the correct answer.

Distractors That Provide Grammatical Cues

When the grammar of a distractor is not parallel in structure to the stem or when the distractor is presented in a different style of language, then students can often pick up on these grammatical cues. For example, in the following item, one of the choices is grammatically inconsistent with the stem:

Example of a Grammatical Cue

Good multiple choice items have which of the following?

A. distractors that are all shorter than the correct answer
B. plausible distractors
C. "all of the above" as a choice
D. avoiding succinct language

Correct answer: B

In this example, the last choice, D, is not consistent with the other choices in grammatical form (it is a gerund, whereas the others are noun phrases). It is also not consistent with the stem as the other choices are. For example, you could repeat back the stem with Choice B like this: "Good multiple choice items have plausible distractors." But you could not do the same for Choice D: "Good multiple choice items have avoiding succinct language." The fact that Choice D is a different part of speech and is also not grammatically consistent with the question can lead students who are testwise to eliminate this choice without ever considering its content.

Grammatical cues that inadvertently point toward a correct answer, in fact, do make an item easier as reported by many studies (Carter, 1986; Dunn & Goldstein, 1959; Evans, 1984; McMorris et al., 1972; Plake & Huntley, 1984; Schmeiser & Whitney, 1973). In addition, when grammatical cues are apparent, item discrimination decreases (Weiten, 1984).

Even adding the subtle grammatical cue of "a(n)" to indicate that an answer could start with either a consonant or a vowel provides information to testwise students. When such a cue is presented in an item and the answer is unknown, students will more often select the answer that starts with a vowel (Plake & Huntley, 1984).

To avoid grammatical cues in choices, several recommendations are to check to make sure all distractors are grammatical with the stem, use parallel syntactic structure, and place articles in the choices.

Distractors with Absolute Words Such as "Always," "Never," "None," and "All"

Many item-writing guides recommend against using determiners such as "always," "never," "none," and "all" (Haladyna, Downing, & Rodriguez, 2002). The definitiveness of these words gives students a clue that the choice is not the correct answer. In a controlled study, Dunn and Goldstein (1959) found that tests that contained items with this cue were easier. Unfortunately, this cue appears frequently in tests. In an analysis of 100 tests written by teachers, specific determiners such as "always" and "never" occurred in 30.5% (Hughes, Salvia, & Bott, 1991). So, the suggested recommendation is to avoid absolute words in the choices.

Choices That Are Not Presented in Logical Order

Generally, the alternatives of a multiple choice item can be placed in a logical order. Numerical values can be arranged from lowest to highest and words can be arranged in alphabetical order. When these logical patterns are violated, research has shown that items tend to be easier (Haladyna & Downing, 1989). Items that become easier because of this pattern indicate that in addition to the knowledge of the content, students are using test-taking strategies to derive the correct answer. Thus, where possible, arrange the choices logically.

Answers in a Consistent Position, Especially the Middle

The context of an answer makes a difference. For example, many instructors write items such that the answer is not at the extremes (A or D), especially if choices are numerical.

Example of Middle Position Bias

How many islands make up the Hawai'ian Islands?

A. 6
B. 7
C. 8
D. 9

Correct answer: C

As evidence that instructors do this, Brozo, Schmelzer and Spires (1984) analyzed 1,220 test items written by college and university instructors and found 79 instances of this pattern. The correct answer appeared in one of the middle positions in 82% of them.

To avoid position bias, some researchers (e.g., Mosier & Price, 1945) have suggested balancing the placement of choices so that the correct answer appears an equal number of times in each position. Suggestions are offered of how to balance the position of choices in Chapter 6.

Since it is recommended that you consciously track where the correct answer appears across all items, you might simplify things at the item writing stage by placing the correct answer first, followed by the distractors. This process, which is recommended by Mosier and Price (1945), will force you to take the explicit step of assigning the position of the correct answers in a deliberate way when you compile the test as a whole. If the choices are all quantities, you might even hold off on creating the distractors until you know the position of the correct answer – this way you will resist the tendency to place the correct answer in the middle of the extremes.

Another issue to consider is whether or not you will be creating alternate forms for your test. The main reason to do this is to deter cheating. If you will be creating alternate forms, then some have suggested using the opportunity to shift around where the answers appear (for example, ordering from ascending to descending in one form and descending to ascending in another). Such shuffling may require extra work in tracking forms, but this process will add to the robustness of the test because the alternate forms will greatly reduce extraneous effects that might be introduced from an answer's position.

This concludes the section of guidelines for writing multiple choice items. You might encounter others in item-writing textbooks, but the guidelines that appear here have all been supported with empirical evidence. For convenience, all the guidelines are summarized in a checklist at the end of the chapter on page 104.

Scoring Multiple Choice Items

The typical approach to scoring multiple choice items is to count responses that match the key as correct and all other responses as incorrect. Researchers have not found much of a benefit to weighting multiple choice items differentially or even using partial credit with multiple choice items. So, just keep it simple.

If you have the ability to tally the responses for each choice including the distractors, this additional information will allow you to do some follow-up analysis on the effectiveness of the distractors. Then, in future items, you might change distractors that were rarely selected or reuse those distractors that were functioning well.

Now that multiple choice has been addressed, we turn to guidelines for other item types.

Guidelines for True/False Items

As we learned previously (in Chapter 3), true/false items are not as effective as multiple choice items. So why is this section in the book at all? Well, it probably shouldn't be. Research has shown that almost every other item type has better psychometric properties, so I again encourage you to use something different. If, however, you are set on using true/false items, this section will provide you with evidence-based guidelines.

The structure of a true/false item is straightforward because it is simply a statement.

Example of a True/False Item

Directions. Read the statement and decide whether it is true or false. If it is true, fill in Circle A on your answer sheet. If it is false, fill in Circle B.

Coal is a renewable source of energy.

Correct answer: False

To avoid ambiguity, the statement is usually about one thing. Consider the following counterexample:

Solar power, which is derived from water pressure, is a renewable source of energy.

Here, there are two propositions: (1) solar power comes from water pressure (which is false), and (2) solar power is a renewable source of energy (which is true). For clarity, the statement should have only one proposition.

The general guidelines for item writing apply to true/false items. As discussed above, these include creating original content, ensuring that items are independent of one another, keeping the language simple, including only relevant material and avoiding words such as "usually" that can add ambiguity.

In addition, several guidelines for multiple choice items apply to true/false items as well. These include being cautious about negative wording, maintaining similar lengths for true and false statements, and avoiding absolute words such as "always." Each of these is discussed below.

Consensus about Negative Wording (T/F)
(It's the Same for Multiple Choice)

Negative wording can be a popular technique in writing true/false questions, for example, "Hydrogen is NOT considered a noble gas." Many researchers suggest that this style of item should be used with caution (Frisbie & Becker, 1991). The reason is that the negative wording can create unnecessary complexity and cognitive load that goes beyond the scope of the test's content. Peterson and Peterson (1976), for example, systematically compared negatively and positively worded true/false items and did indeed observe more errors with negatively worded items compared to positively worded items. This finding is consistent with research on multiple choice items as well. In a review of textbooks that discuss item writing, 31 out of 35 authors recommended that negative wording should be avoided (Haladyna & Downing, 1989).

Longer Statements Tend to Be True

It appears to be common knowledge that longer statements tend to be true. Although I was not able to locate a study that corroborates this finding, it seems logical. In multiple choice items, the pattern clearly exists: the correct choice tends to be longer than the distractors (a finding that has been verified by Brozo et al. (1984)). Again the reason most likely is that item writers have to ensure that the statement is true, which requires more description. To avoid a situation where students are able to guess the correct answer from testwiseness, a suggestion is to try to keep the lengths of true and false statements equivalent.

Absolute Words Tend to Be False

Absolute words such as "all," "always," "never," and "only" give students a clue that the statement is probably false because absolutes tend to have exceptions. A test-wise guide by Putman (2015) states, "assume false if the item uses absolute words; you can usually find an exception to an absolute statement." For this reason, researchers suggest avoiding absolute terms (Kubiszyn & Borich, 2003).

Be Conscious of the Total Number of True Answers

It has been documented by several researchers that there is a distinct tendency for students to select "true" more often than "false" when guessing (Cronbach, 1942; Gustav, 1963). The implication of this is that items that are false have been shown to be more reliable and more valid than items that are true (Cronbach, 1942). Does this mean that you should include more false items in your test? Some do draw this conclusion, but the conundrum is that students also are very adept at detecting patterns in answer keys (Evans, 1984) and will most definitely start to realize that your tendency as an item writer is to include more false items in your test compared to true items. The important step is to be aware of these two findings: that students tend to guess "true" and that students can pick up on patterns in answer keys.

Scoring True/False Items

Scoring true/false items will be straightforward. Usually true will be assigned to A on a machine-scoring sheet and false will be assigned to B. If students are writing answers directly onto the test, you might consider typing out "T   F" before each item and have students respond by circling the letter. This approach helps avoid any issues of legibility from handwriting or changed answers.

Scoring of an Alternate True/False Item Type

There is a special type of true/false item that is called Type X by the National Board of Medical Examiners. In this item, the student is presented with a scenario and four subitems, such as the following:

> Which food type would be limited for a patient with pre-diabetes?
>
> I.   Bread
> II. Milk
> III. Cupcakes
> IV. Chicken

Then for each subitem, the student is asked to make a true/false decision. There are different ways that such an item-type might be scored. For example, you could mark the item correct only if all four subanswers are correct, you could offer partial credit, or you could consider each subitem a separate item. Research indicates that treating each subitem as an independent true/false item is the best approach because it increases reliability (Albanese & Sabers, 1978; Albanese, Kent, & Whitney, 1979).

Guidelines for Matching Items

The medical field has long made use of the matching format in formal examinations because these items perform well from a psychometric standpoint and can be written to measure higher cognitive functioning (Case & Swanson, 1998).

Because students have most likely been doing matching exercises since childhood and because many formats require lines to be drawn for the matching, the directions should describe explicitly how the matching should be indicated. Often, you'll be asking students to fill in the correct choice on an answer sheet.

Some educators (Kubiszyn & Borich, 2010) have suggested placing the longer descriptions in the left-hand column (Column A) as in the following example:

Example of a Matching Item

Directions. There are two columns. Column A lists
descriptions of experiments. Column B lists statistical
analyses. On the line next to each description, write
the letter of the statistical analysis that best matches
the experiment. A letter may be selected once,
multiple times, or not at all.

Column A		Column B
1. Reaction times are collected under two conditions: one with pictures that prime a word and one with pictures that are unrelated. Each subject is randomly assigned to a condition. The researcher wants to see if the reaction times of the two conditions are significantly different from one another. ___	A B C D	2x3 ANOVA Chi square Independent samples t-test Kappa
2. Two raters are making intelligibility judgments about the speech of 100 non-native speakers. The researcher wants to know how well the judgments of the two raters match. ___	E	Paired samples t-test

Correct answers: C, D

The reason for placing the long descriptions in Column A
has to do with the intuition of how students approach

matching items. Generally, what a student will do is read the first item in Column A and then scan through the choices in Column B to identify the best match. If the more lengthy descriptions are listed in Column B, it will take the student longer to complete the items.

Include More Choices Than Descriptions

A survey of teacher-made tests revealed that test-writing errors were most common on matching items (Pigge & Marso, 1988). One common error is to provide the same number of choices as descriptions. With this format, the student can narrow down the choices through the process of elimination.

Allow Choices to Be Selected More Than Once

On a related note, if choices can be used only once and a student determines that a specific choice fits with one description the best (even though it might be a possible match with other descriptions), then the student can confidently disregard this choice for future items. Thus, it is important not only to offer more choices, but to allow students to select a choice as the answer for more than one description.

Some other guidelines can be generalized from multiple choice item writing, such as arranging the choices in logical order (for example, alphabetically), avoiding choices that share critical keywords with a description, and avoiding choices that can be eliminated because of grammatical cues.

Scoring Matching Items

There are different ways to address scoring on matching items. For example, a set of five descriptions and seven choices could be considered one item. If a student gets three of the five correct, then the item would be scored either wrong or partially correct. Alternatively, each description could be considered a separate item (in which case, the student would get three correct and two incorrect). From a psychometric perspective, it is better to treat each description as a separate item. Even if you are scoring with partial credit, having more items is better for reliability.

Guidelines for Open-Ended Items

According to some surveys, open-ended items have been shown to be used more frequently than even multiple choice items (at least at the high school level) (Fleming & Chambers, 1983). The format is very straight-forward. There is a question and a space for the student to write in a single-word answer or short phrase.

Frankly, I was not able to find much research supporting or debunking specific guidelines on how to write these items. Apparently, other researchers have found the same to be true. In a review of 25 textbooks and chapters on item writing, Hogan and Murphy (2007) found that most guidelines for writing constructed-response items lacked empirical evidence. So, I default to common knowledge published in item writing texts.

Elicit Constrained Responses

The main challenge for writing open-ended items is to avoid ambiguity and elicit a constrained answer. Consider the following item:

> When did Obama become president of the United States?

A student might write a response of "January" or "the late 2000s." Yes, technically presidents are sworn in on January 20th, and yes, 2009 is in the late 2000s, but the item writer was probably looking for a year. The item might be rewritten like this, "In which year did Obama first become president of the United States?" As a reminder, try to extend beyond rote knowledge with these items.

Other than this tip of eliciting constrained responses, the popular guidelines I have come across for this item type apply to tests in general and are addressed in other sections of this chapter.

Scoring Open-Ended Items

The first issue surrounding the scoring of open-ended items is that a student may come up with an answer that is correct, or partially correct, but unanticipated. With this type of item, it is common to accept multiple correct answers. If you feel that an answer should be marked as correct after the fact, then if practicing standardized scoring, you should change the answer key and give credit to all tests with the same answer. Sometimes a response may be correct, but it misses the point of the item. If the item can be revised to avoid ambiguity, it might be best just to accept the response as correct and improve the item for a future test.

One of the questions that arises when scoring open-ended items is whether or not a student's score should be reduced because of spelling or grammatical errors. This is a matter of opinion. Since a misspelled item is not completely correct, there is a clear reason why the student should receive only partial credit for such an answer. However, in large-scale assessments that target content mastery such as Advanced Placement exams, grammar and spelling errors do not affect scores as long as a grader can unambiguously determine what a word is intended to be.

Generally, awarding partial credit for open-ended items is a good thing. In comparisons of tests which allowed partial credit with those that were only scored correct or incorrect, partial credit resulted in better reliability (DeMars, 2008). That said, precise scoring guidelines should specify exactly when an answer should receive partial versus full credit.

Guidelines for Essays

As with open-ended items, I was not able to find much empirical evidence surrounding best practices on writing prompts for essays. What follows are some general guidelines from the literature (some with and some without support).

Offering a Choice of Prompts

Although advice is divided on whether or not to offer students several prompts and allow them to choose which to respond to, some empirical evidence suggests that it is beneficial to offer this choice. In one study, students wrote several essays and indicated the ones they preferred to have selected for their final score. Not surprisingly, scores on the preferred essays were higher than the essays not preferred (Bridgeman, Morgan, & Wang, 1996). Of more interest is that the preferred essays had a higher correlation with an outside criterion, indicating that the validity of the preferred essays was better. A counter argument to offering choices is that students will be graded on different items, which may reduce reliability (although I was not able to find a specific study that addressed this topic).

Providing Focusing Information and a Clear Purpose

One guideline is to include a focus statement that briefly orients students to the topic of the essay (Calfee &

Miller, 2007). The benefit of doing so is that the focusing material provides some context for the student's responses.

Next, it is recommended that a prompt include a clear purpose of the essay (Calfee & Miller, 2007). An ambiguous prompt will make grading more difficult because different essays may address different aspects of a concept. With a clear purpose, you will help guide students toward the material you want them to explore.

Using Action Verbs

Some suggestions for what to ask students to do in an essay are compare and contrast, arrive at conclusions, explain causes and effects, evaluate a viewpoint, support an argument, or point out strengths and weaknesses (Kubiszyn & Borich, 2010).

When choosing a verb to instruct students on what to do, some have suggested basing these verbs on levels of Bloom's Taxonomy (Anderson & Krathwohl, 2001). For example, for Comprehension, you might use verbs such as *describe* and *restate*; and for higher levels of thought, you might use verbs such as *evaluate, diagnose,* and *propose.*

Specifying How Long the Essay Should Be

Another guideline is to specify the recommended length of the essay (Haladyna & Rodriguez, 2013), for example, "The essay should be no longer than a page," or "In three or four paragraphs, compare and contrast ...." Length constraints will help students plan how many points and supporting details to cover and manage their time appropriately.

Scoring Essays

The essay scoring process will be greatly influenced by your philosophical approach on how to assign grades in general. The most popular way to score essays in today's age is to use a criterion-referenced approach in which the essay is rated against an established set of standards. These standards are specified in a rubric, which is a list of specific criteria that will be considered in the grading process.

An alternative is to score essays according to a group-referenced approach in which scores depend on how a student performed in relation to other students in the class. Teachers often describe creating piles as they read essays: one pile for exceptional essays, one for satisfactory essays, and a third for the worst essays. Essentially, the instructor uses these piles to rank order the essays, and this ordering is then the basis for assigning grades.

There are several advantages of using a rubric. First, with rubrics, grades are easier to justify to students. You can sit down with the student and explain why an essay met the requirements of one level of performance but not the next tier. In contrast, it is more difficult to explain why the student's essay was ranked lower than another student's, especially when you have returned all the essays, and when these rankings were based on your intuitions. Even if your intuitions are spot on (since you have years of experience reading essays and have by now developed a keen sense for what makes for a good essay or bad essay), the student will most likely find it more satisfying to find reasons in a tangible rubric as opposed to an abstraction of your experience. And who is to say whether or not the student would be ranked the same if the student were to take the test in a class the following year with different students.

The second advantage of using a rubric is that it improves reliability. A meta-analysis of 75 empirical research studies on the effectiveness of rubrics showed that rubrics do improve scoring reliability (Jonsson & Svingby, 2007). Professional organizations also support the use of rubrics.

Rubrics when used, are often given to students before the exam. This way, students understand what the expectations are for different levels of performance. So, while you are in the process of writing essay prompts, it is a good idea to start thinking about your rubric (if you choose to use one).

Writing Rubrics

Some rubrics are holistic, in that they have the grader think of the essay as a whole and suggest a score based on pre-established levels. Others are analytic in that they break down the judgments into a number of criteria, which are usually traits such as *Content* or *Organization*. Then the essay is scored according to each criterion independently. Table 5-1 presents an example of a generic analytic rubric for essay scoring that emphasizes content mastery (as opposed to writing skills).

Table 5-1. Example of a Writing Rubric for Essay Scoring

	Level 1: Far Below Expectations	Level 2: Below Expectations	Level 3: Meets Expectations	Level 4: Exceeds Expectations
Content Mastery (60%)	The points raised were not relevant to the prompt. Most of the appropriate information was omitted or misrepresented.	The points in the essay were somewhat relevant to the prompt. Some important information was missing or addressed superficially.	The points raised were relevant. The prompt was fully or almost fully addressed, although some information might have been more precise or synthesized better.	The points raised were relevant to the prompt. The information conveyed was precise and demonstrated complex thinking.

	Level 1: Far Below Expectations	Level 2: Below Expectations	Level 3: Meets Expectations	Level 4: Exceeds Expectations
Supporting Details (32%)	There was insufficient supporting evidence for the claims made in the essay.	Some supporting evidence was provided; however, some key concepts were not supported or were supported superficially or with irrelevant information.	All claims in the essay were supported with sufficient evidence, although the evidence could have been more thorough or convincing.	All claims in the essay were supported thoroughly with convincing evidence.
Conventions (8%)	There were substantial spelling, grammar, punctuation, and/or formatting errors. These errors interfered with the content and readability of the essay.	Frequent spelling, grammar, punctuation, and/or formatting errors did not interfere with the content of the essay, but did disrupt the essay's flow.	Some spelling, grammar, punctuation or formatting errors were present, but these errors did not detract from the essay's content or flow.	Spelling, grammar, punctuation, and formatting errors were extremely rare.

You can design your own rubric with traits specific to the skills and abilities you want your students to master.

As indicated by the rubric above, Content Mastery is 60%, Supporting Details is 32%, and Conventions is 8%. Using the rubric, an instructor would rate each trait on a scale from 1 to 4, based on the level. As an example, the instructor might score a Level 3 for Content Mastery, a Level 4 for Supporting Details and a Level 3 for Conventions. To map the Content Mastery Level to the subscore, multiply by 15 (Level 4 x 15 would equal 60 possible points). Multiply by 8 for Supporting Details and by 2 for Conventions. The total score for this essay would then be the following:

3 on Content Mastery x 15 =	45 pts. (out of 60 pts.)
4 on Supporting Details x 8 =	32 pts. (out of 32 pts.)
3 on Conventions x 2 =	6 pts. (out of 8 pts.)
Essay Score	83 pts. (out of 100 pts.)

This is just an example. You can change the scoring algorithm to fit your own style of rubric.

Test Scoring

"Test scoring that involves human judgment should include rubrics, procedures, and criteria for scoring."

- AERA, APA, & NCME, 2014
Standard 6.8

If your test contains short essays, often instructors do not use a full-blown rubric, but rather include in the prompt a description of how the response will be scored. The following is an example.

Example of Describing Scoring Criteria in an Essay Prompt

"... In your essay, provide at least two examples to support your argument. You will be graded equally on content, organization, and mechanics including spelling and grammar. (15 points)"

More detail about the process of scoring essays is discussed in Chapter 9. The important steps here are to define how you will be scoring the essays so that your approach is available and transparent to students.

Now that we have gone through general item writing guidelines for different item types, it is time to put these guidelines into practice. The following checklists are provided so that while you are writing items you can view the guidelines at a glance. Happy item writing.

Summary of Item Writing Guidelines

General Guidelines

- [ ] Create original content.
- [ ] Write items that are independent of one another.
- [ ] Keep the language simple.
- [ ] Keep the items succinct.
- [ ] Avoid words such as "often" that can add ambiguity.

Multiple Choice

- [ ] Use a complete sentence or question in the stem.
- [ ] Use negation only when necessary.
- [ ] Write only two or three distractors.
- [ ] Avoid complex choices such as "A and B but not C."
- [ ] Avoid "all of the above."
- [ ] Avoid "none of the above."
- [ ] Place choices in logical order.

Avoid testwise clues including the following:

- [ ] -Related choices or choices that are the opposite.
- [ ] -Answers that are the longest choice.
- [ ] -Answers with keywords shared with the stem.
- [ ] -Answers that are the most general choice.
- [ ] -Distractors that are not grammatical with the stem.
- [ ] -Distractors with absolute words such as "always."

True/False

- [ ] Use negation only when necessary.
- [ ] Keep the length of true and false statements similar.
- [ ] Avoid absolute words such as "always" and "never."

Matching

- [ ] Include more choices than descriptions.
- [ ] Allow choices to be selected more than once.
- [ ] List choices in a logical order.
- [ ] Don't place a keyword from a description in a choice.
- [ ] Ensure all choices are grammatical with the descriptions.

Open-Ended

- [ ] Write items so that they elicit constrained responses.

Essays

- [ ] Include initial focusing information in the prompt.
- [ ] Write a clear purpose of the essay.
- [ ] Use action verbs that elicit appropriate thinking.
- [ ] Specify a recommended length of the essay.
- [ ] Make available to students the scoring criteria/rubric.

CHAPTER 6:

Reviewing the Test

Now that you have created test items, it is time to bring them together for a final review. There will be several review steps. The first is to review items and choose the ones that will appear on the test. If you created more items than you will need, now is the time to decide which to keep and which to throw out or save for a different time. Use your test blueprint as a guide to help you determine how many questions of different levels of difficulty you need for each content area and vet those within the appropriate levels. Set aside discarded items for now because you may need to swap in one or two if another item needs to be tossed out for a different reason such as duplicate content or potential bias.

After you assemble all the items together into a test form, it is a good idea to review not just the items but the test as a whole so that you can see how the items flow from one to the next. You might need to modify the order or replace some if you notice items that are too similar to one another. This chapter discusses each of these review steps in turn.

Reviewing Your Items

When you review your test items, you'll want to switch hats and view them objectively through the eyes of the student (as opposed to the item writer). Remember, for an item to be good, it should meet the following criteria:

(1) The item should have the appropriate content.

(2) Ideally, the item should be answered correctly by students who have mastered the content and be answered incorrectly by students who have not.

(3) The item should be free from clues that are more related to good test-taking skills than the content of the test.

(4) The item should be fair and without bias.

If possible, also consider having another expert such as a graduate teaching assistant or another instructor review the items. The following are different perspectives to take during your review.

Review for Validity

The first step in the review process is to take steps toward avoiding threats to validity. As discussed in detail during item writing, a major challenge for validity is construct-irrelevant variance; that is, differences in performances that are due to something other than what the test is designed to measure.

One of the main factors that can increase construct-irrelevant variance is to create an advantage for test-savvy students due to the way test questions are written, not what they are about. There are many research studies that show how students undoubtedly learn patterns and pick up on subtle cues on tests (Dolly & Williams, 1986; Evans, 1984; Sarnacki, 1979). An advantage for you is that empirically-based cues have been covered in this book.

Now, as a reviewer (instead of an item writer), critically analyze your items to see if a test-savvy student could answer any questions correctly without knowing the content:

- Do any items give away answers to other items?

- Can the item be answered based on general knowledge as opposed to knowledge of course content?

Also review items for common mistakes that were covered previously in Chapter 5: Writing Items. The points specific to avoiding construct-irrelevant variance are repeated here for convenience.

For multiple choice items:

- Does the item include the choice "all of the above," which is often selected by testwise students?

- Is the correct answer the opposite of another choice or can it be derived from a convergence strategy?

- Is the correct answer the longest choice?

- Does the correct answer contain a keyword that is also in the stem?

- Is the correct answer revealed because it is more general than the other choices?

- Can choices be eliminated because they are grammatically inconsistent with the stem?

- Can a distractor be eliminated because it contains an absolute word such as "all," "none," "always," or "never"?

- Are choices listed illogically when they could follow a logical order (such as smallest to largest)?

For true/false items:

- Are there patterns such as a tendency for true statements to be longer than false statements?

- Do false statements contain absolute words such as "all," none," always," or "never"?

For matching items:

- Are there an equal number of descriptions and choices (which would allow test-savvy students to eliminate choices)?

- Are choices used only once (which would also allow test-savvy students to eliminate choices)?

- Are choices listed illogically when they could follow a logical order (such as alphabetically)?

- Does a choice contain a keyword that is also in a description?

- Can choices be eliminated because they are grammatically inconsistent with descriptions?

Fortunately, constructed-response items are less susceptible to testwiseness strategies.

Review for Fairness

Finally, the items should be reviewed for fairness. In test development, it is best to screen items before the test is in front of the student. Consider reviewing for material that is taboo, potentially biased, stereotypical toward disadvantaged groups, offensive, or emotionally charged.

Some examples of topics to avoid include the following (listed alphabetically):

- Abortion
- Abuse (child, domestic)
- Addiction, alcohol, drugs, substance abuse
- Aliens, ESP, paranormal phenomenon
- Bodily functions, nudity
- Creationism, evolution
- Debt, financial hardship, losing a job, unemployment
- Death, disease, health problems, smoking
- Disrespectful behavior, quarreling
- Gambling
- Gay marriage
- Genocide, hate crimes, racism
- Gun control, guns, weapons
- Physical attributes (beauty/ugliness, cosmetic surgery, weight)
- Political preferences, political figures who are controversial
- Religion (Atheism, Christianity, Islam, Judaism, references to God, etc.)
- Sex, sexual harassment, sexual orientation

- Socio-economic inequalities (assuming access to consumer goods, gadgets, large homes, luxury cars, privileged activities)

- Stereotypes (cultural, ethnic, and gender)

- Unlawful behavior, gangs

- Violence, gore

- Witchcraft

Of course some of these topics might be important for your content domain. If they are, then take time to review the language in your items that might be interpreted as offensive.

Bias reviews also include screening out cultural references that extend beyond the content of the course material and that students from other countries might not be expected to know, for example, certain holidays, slang, or popular movies or music.

Review for Difficulty Due to Language

In addition to screening out items that might be offensive to some students, items also should be reviewed for unnecessarily difficult language that is not related to course content. All items can be reviewed for the following:

- Is the language unnecessarily difficult, especially for non-native speakers?

- Is there negative wording that might obscure the meaning of the question?

- Are acronyms and/or abbreviations used that are not relevant to the course content?

A certain level of content-specific vocabulary might be necessary for demonstrating mastery of your course content. That said, the authors of the *Standards* strongly recommend that language demands on a test be minimized (unless it is a language test) (p. 64). Otherwise, the test will also be assessing language knowledge and use.

The style of language used in items is a hot topic in the field of testing and was given more attention in the most recent 2014 version of the *Standards* (compared to the previous version from 1999). The *Standards* states that "the level of language proficiency ... required by the test should be kept to the minimum required ... to represent the target construct(s)" (AERA, APA, & NCME, 2014). The issue is not one to overlook, especially since the topic has been the source of litigation in the past.

Aligning with the Test Blueprint

It is very likely that you will decide not to use a handful of items as a result of your review. This is to be expected and encouraged. By choosing only the best items, you are ensuring high test quality. At this point in the process, you might consider going back to your test blueprint to bring your numbers in alignment with your original plan. It is okay to make modifications at this point, but if possible, try to fill any gaps by generating new items. Importantly, you want to be sure that the final test reflects what is specified in the test blueprint.

Compiling Your Test

Now, it is time to bring everything together into a final test layout including directions, point values, and items.

There are several tips that are relevant at this stage. Most are not thoroughly investigated in the literature, but they make sense, nonetheless. One of these is to make sure all parts of a question appear on the same page so that students do not need to waste time flipping back and forth between pages (Kaplan & Saccuzzo, 2013).

Another recommendation is to present items of the same format together on the test. This suggestion makes sense logically since each item type will have a different set of directions and will most likely be scored in the same way.

Another suggestion is to state the point value at the beginning of each test section (Kaplan & Saccuzzo, 2013). The point value makes the scoring transparent and allows students to use this information for time management during the testing session. Your blueprint might be a useful guide when compiling your test because it will remind you of how many points you initially planned to award for each test section.

Writing Directions

It may appear unnecessary to write out what the student needs to do on a test because it seems so intuitive, but it is important from the viewpoint of fairness to provide clear instructions. All test takers should have access to the same information about how to do each task.

Some suggestions for simple directions for each type of item follow. These are just examples and should be rewritten to suit the needs of your own test.

Multiple Choice

Example Multiple Choice Directions

"For each item, select the one best answer and fill in the appropriate circle on your answer sheet."

Some researchers have recommended that the directions for multiple choice items mention the "best" choice or answer as opposed to the "correct" choice or answer because the word "best" is more defensible if challenged (Downing, 2006).

True/False

Example True/False Directions

"Read each statement and decide whether it is true or false. On your answer sheet, fill in A if you think the statement is true. Fill in B if you think the statement is false."

A common sense suggestion is to use an answer sheet or have the student circle T/F on a handout – this way poor handwriting will not introduce any response ambiguity.

Matching

Example Matching Directions

"There are two columns. Column A lists [description of what it lists]. Column B lists [description of what it lists]. On your answer sheet, fill in the letter from Column B that best matches the description in Column A. A choice may be selected once, multiple times, or not at all."

As with the multiple choice directions, a suggestion is to use the word "best" when describing the choices.

Open-Ended

Example Open-Ended Directions

"In the space provided write a word or phrase that best answers the question."

Since math problems are often in the open-ended format, it can sometimes be difficult to find the final answer among all the work the student has done. One way around this is to provide a blank area for work space and below this insert a box where the student can write the final answer.

Essay

Essay prompts usually include the directions in the prompt itself.

Example Essay Directions

"… In the space provided, you should address all parts of the question and support your arguments with details. Spelling and grammatical errors will not count against you. The attached rubric will be used in scoring. You will have 20 minutes to write your essay. (10 points)"

Estimating Time

As the test creator, timing yourself on the test will probably not give you a representative estimate of the amount of time it will take students to finish. However, timing yourself will give you some idea of how long it might take an extremely proficient student to read through all the instructions and questions and record answers. Some testing centers have recommended timing yourself on the exam and then multiplying this number by 4 or by 6 (Center for Educational Innovation, 2015). Others have suggested 30 seconds for simple questions, one minute for more complex questions, and even more time for questions that tap higher-order thinking such as analyzing, evaluating, and synthesizing (Faculty Center for Teaching and Learning, 2015). Looking at time allotments in large-scale assessments from ETS and ACT, it seems that students are generally given 20-25 minutes for in-depth essays and 10-15 minutes for shorter essays. The best way to determine the optimum number of questions is experience from administering prior exams.

Numbering Items

Research suggests that all items should be numbered to avoid confusion (Kaplan & Saccuzzo, 2013). Along these lines, repeated numbering in which the numbering starts over at each section might introduce some ambiguity. Do teachers make these kinds of errors? The answer is yes. In an analysis of teacher-written tests, 17% of the tests did not number items consecutively (Pigge & Marso, 1988).

Placing Correct Answers in Multiple Choice Items

Although item writers may think they are placing answer choices evenly across choice positions (A, B, C, or D), analysis of actual tests shows a different pattern. Specifically, multiple choice answers tend to be placed in position C most often and D least often (Attali and Bar-Hillel, 2003; McNamara & Weitzman, 1945). Further, students are amazingly adept at picking up on a teacher's preference for placing answers in a specific position. Several studies have shown that when a test has a high frequency of items with the correct answer in a specific slot, students have a tendency to guess that position when they do not know the answer (Jones & Kaufman, 1975; Wevrick, 1962). Other research clearly shows that students learn the patterns of correct answer placement from tests written by their instructors (Evans, 1984).

The take-away from all of this is that you should not be an open book. Don't let your students detect your patterns and exploit them to get a better test score. One way to deal with this is to balance the placement of correct answers and distractors. Balancing distractors is important, too. As Mosier and Price (1945) describe, "since distracters tend to be written in order of plausibility, with the last distracter often written as a desperate final effort, a randomization process should extend beyond the correct choice to the incorrect ones as well."

Mosier and Price (1945) offer a randomization method for multiple choice tests with items containing five choices. Since five choices is not recommended, the following are three randomizers for items with four choices and three choices, respectively (there are three tables for each so that your randomization pattern across tests is not always the same). If you have more items than listed in the table, simply go to the next table.

Table 6-1. Randomizer for Items with Four Choices

	Answer	Distractor 1	Distractor 2	Distractor 3
Item 1	D	A	C	B
Item 2	D	B	A	C
Item 3	A	B	D	C
Item 4	C	A	B	D
Item 5	C	D	A	B
Item 6	C	D	B	A
Item 7	B	D	A	C
Item 8	A	D	C	B
Item 9	D	C	B	A
Item 10	D	B	C	A
Item 11	B	C	A	D
Item 12	C	B	A	D
Item 13	B	A	D	C
Item 14	A	B	C	D
Item 15	C	A	D	B
Item 16	B	A	C	D
Item 17	A	C	D	B
Item 18	B	D	C	A
Item 19	C	B	D	A
Item 20	A	C	B	D
Item 21	D	A	B	C
Item 22	B	C	D	A
Item 23	A	D	B	C
Item 24	D	C	A	B

Table 6-2. Another Randomizer for Items with Four Choices

	Answer	Distractor 1	Distractor 2	Distractor 3
Item 1	D	A	B	C
Item 2	A	C	B	D
Item 3	B	C	A	D
Item 4	A	B	C	D
Item 5	B	C	D	A
Item 6	C	D	A	B
Item 7	C	B	A	D
Item 8	C	A	D	B
Item 9	B	A	C	D
Item 10	A	C	D	B
Item 11	B	D	A	C
Item 12	C	A	B	D
Item 13	B	A	D	C
Item 14	C	B	D	A
Item 15	D	C	A	B
Item 16	C	D	B	A
Item 17	D	B	C	A
Item 18	B	D	C	A
Item 19	D	C	B	A
Item 20	A	D	C	B
Item 21	A	D	B	C
Item 22	A	B	D	C
Item 23	D	A	C	B
Item 24	D	B	A	C

Table 6-3. Yet Another Randomizer for Items with Four Choices

	Answer	Distractor 1	Distractor 2	Distractor 3
Item 1	C	A	D	B
Item 2	A	B	C	D
Item 3	A	C	B	D
Item 4	A	B	D	C
Item 5	C	D	B	A
Item 6	C	B	D	A
Item 7	D	A	C	B
Item 8	D	C	B	A
Item 9	B	C	A	D
Item 10	D	B	A	C
Item 11	B	A	D	C
Item 12	C	B	A	D
Item 13	B	D	C	A
Item 14	B	C	D	A
Item 15	D	A	B	C
Item 16	B	D	A	C
Item 17	C	D	A	B
Item 18	D	B	C	A
Item 19	A	D	B	C
Item 20	D	C	A	B
Item 21	A	D	C	B
Item 22	B	A	C	D
Item 23	C	A	B	D
Item 24	A	C	D	B

Table 6-4. Randomizer for Items with Three Choices

	Answer	Distractor 1	Distractor 2
Item 1	C	A	B
Item 2	B	C	A
Item 3	B	C	A
Item 4	B	C	A
Item 5	A	B	C
Item 6	A	C	B
Item 7	B	A	C
Item 8	A	B	C
Item 9	C	B	A
Item 10	C	B	A
Item 11	A	C	B
Item 12	C	A	B
Item 13	B	A	C
Item 14	C	B	A
Item 15	C	A	B
Item 16	B	A	C
Item 17	A	B	C
Item 18	C	A	B
Item 19	A	C	B
Item 20	B	A	C
Item 21	A	B	C
Item 22	C	B	A
Item 23	A	C	B
Item 24	B	C	A

Table 6-5. Another Randomizer for Items with Three Choices

	Answer	Distractor 1	Distractor 2
Item 1	B	A	C
Item 2	A	C	B
Item 3	B	A	C
Item 4	B	C	A
Item 5	A	C	B
Item 6	B	A	C
Item 7	B	A	C
Item 8	C	B	A
Item 9	A	B	C
Item 10	C	A	B
Item 11	C	B	A
Item 12	B	C	A
Item 13	B	C	A
Item 14	A	C	B
Item 15	A	B	C
Item 16	A	B	C
Item 17	B	C	A
Item 18	C	B	A
Item 19	C	A	B
Item 20	C	A	B
Item 21	A	B	C
Item 22	A	C	B
Item 23	C	A	B
Item 24	C	B	A

Table 6-6. Yet Another Randomizer for Items with Three Choices

	Answer	Distractor 1	Distractor 2
Item 1	C	B	A
Item 2	A	C	B
Item 3	C	A	B
Item 4	A	B	C
Item 5	C	A	B
Item 6	B	C	A
Item 7	A	C	B
Item 8	B	A	C
Item 9	B	A	C
Item 10	B	C	A
Item 11	C	A	B
Item 12	B	C	A
Item 13	B	C	A
Item 14	A	B	C
Item 15	A	B	C
Item 16	A	C	B
Item 17	A	C	B
Item 18	B	A	C
Item 19	C	B	A
Item 20	A	B	C
Item 21	C	B	A
Item 22	B	A	C
Item 23	C	B	A
Item 24	C	A	B

If you do not want your answer key published in a book, you can go to the following website to generate your own random order: http://www.intelliphonics.com/source/randomizer.html

If you have more items than listed in the table, simply generate another table. If you are using three choices instead of four, you can use the table by disregarding the D choice.

Avoiding Patterns in Answer Keys

William Poundstone, author of *Rock Breaks Scissors: A Practical Guide to Outguessing and Outwitting Almost Everybody* (2014), collected 100 tests from a range of sources and then analyzed these tests for statistical patterns. One of his findings was that the letters of the correct answers rarely repeated consecutively. For example, an answer key is more likely to be

A D A B C B A B C D C D

as opposed to

A A A C B D D D C C B B.

A possible reason for this is that humans have a perception of what randomness is, which is not actually correct (Williams & Griffiths, 2013). In our subconscious minds, randomness does not repeat as often. The downside to this is that any student who has read Poundstone's book will be able to guess a correct answer by eliminating letter choices from surrounding items. For example, if the student is not sure of the answer for Item 2, but the student is confident that the answer to Item 1 is B and the answer to Item 3 is A, then the test taker has a clue that the correct choice for Item 2 will be C or D. If you used the randomizer method above, then this issue should be addressed already. If you did not use a randomizer, then don't be afraid to keep some strings of the same letter in there.

Lack of repetition in answer keys also applies to true/false items. Do not be afraid to include strings of true answers and strings of false answers in your key.

Creating Alternate Forms

There are both pros and cons to creating more than one form of your test. The downside, of course, is the extra time it will take to produce another form, create another grading key, and sort through who was given which form. Alternate forms do have considerable benefits though. The main advantage is to deter cheating. The sad truth is that the majority of students in college cheat (Diekhoff, et al., 1996; Gardner, Roper, Gonzalez, & Simpson, 1988; McCabe, 1992). Granted, this is probably no surprise since rampant cheating is exactly the reason instructors have to create new tests each year, as items will undoubtedly find their way into the hands of the next set of students taking a course. To help discourage cheating, alternate forms can be created that scramble the order of items and the position of choices. These alternate forms will present confusing information to cheaters who cannot help but to take a quick peek at a neighbor's answer sheet. In the item writing chapters, there were guidelines with recommendations regarding how choices should be presented (in logical order). Inverting the order of choices (for example from largest to smallest instead of smallest to largest) will still allow for logical ordering. Just be sure that you are meticulous about labeling the forms and creating appropriate scoring keys for each form.

Other advantages of using alternate forms include reducing order effects (from some items always following other items), and canceling out positional preferences of correct answers (if answer positions are shuffled).

Reviewing Your Test

Now it is time to review your test as a whole. As with item reviews, there are several perspectives to consider.

Review the Basic Layout

Take a quick look at the layout of the test and go through each of these questions:

- Are there items that span multiple pages? If so, then this can cause extra burden on the test takers not related to the content of the test.

- Are all the pages numbered?

- Are all the items numbered consecutively?

- Do all sections have directions?

- Do all sections specify the point value for each item?

- If there are essay questions, is the student's name concealed so that biases in grading can be avoided? (This topic is discussed in detail in Chapter 9.)

Review for Validity

The first step in the test review process is to examine validity. A test is considered invalid if it is not measuring what it is intended to measure. The two most relevant kinds of validity evidence for purposes of assigning grades are construct validity evidence and content validity evidence.

What would a student's perspective of the test's validity be? Does this test appear to be measuring what it is intended to measure? What arguments might someone make suggesting that it is not relevant or does not allow students to show their mastery of the course material? Make sure that you can answer these questions to ensure the validity of your test.

Now, think of the test in terms of content validity. Does the content in the test items reflect what is represented on the test blueprint? Do the items accurately depict the important content areas that you have been emphasizing in the course? Could a student potentially complain that the items on the test did not align with the content in the course? Does the test allow for higher-level thinking expected of your students at this stage in their educational careers? If you can make defensible arguments for each of these points, then you most likely have some evidence for the content validity of the test.

Review for Reliability

Reliability describes a test's consistency. The key point to remember about reliability is that the more measurements you collect from your students, the more confident you can be of the overall measurement's precision. As a general guideline, the more items you include in a test, the more reliable it will be. So, the main question to ask is whether or not there are enough items. The tradeoffs are time limitations and potential for fatigue.

If you feel that your test could use a few more items to bolster the reliability, now is the time to make these additions.

Review for Fairness

In the test review process, you already did an extensive review of potential bias of individual items. When reviewing the test as a whole, you can review the items for bias once more and also check if some subgroups (e.g., males versus females) are disproportionately represented across the test. If you make up names of characters for your items ("Peter is calculating the reliability of a standardized test ..."), you can try to balance the gender of the characters across items and introduce names from different cultures.

Done - The Final Product

Now after considerable work, your final product should be a quality test. The test should be aligned with your test blueprint, which will ensure good representation of content for validity and a sufficient number of items for reliability. Your careful item writing should help you avoid construct-irrelevant variance and your careful reviews should ensure fairness. Don't stop here, though. Quality administration and scoring are important for validity, too. From here are discussions of how to prepare your students, how to standardize your test administration, and how to ensure valid and fair scoring.

CHAPTER 7:

Preparing Students for the Test

The theme of this chapter is setting expectations. Some institutions and instructors now require students to read formal documentation at the beginning of a course so that students are well aware of what to expect and formally agree to the course assumptions and rules. By setting expectations, you greatly reduce later conflict related to testing and course grades.

Also, students have rights and responsibilities that they need to be aware of. For example, all students have a right to the confidentiality of their test results. They also have responsibilities, such as, not disclosing questions from the test to anyone. By going through not just the expected content of the test, but also rights and responsibilities, you set expectations as to what is and is not acceptable in the testing process.

Set Expectations about Content

Students have a basic right to be informed about the general nature of the test, how it will be administered, how it will be graded, and how it impacts final grades. The idea is to give enough guidance about the exam so that students can prepare themselves and so that the results accurately reflect their mastery of the course material.

On the other hand, you do not want to provide too much information and jeopardize the validity of the test scores. Using practice items that are too similar to test items may artificially improve test scores.

Use and Interpretation of Educational Assessments

"In educational settings, test users should take steps to prevent test preparation activities and distribution of materials to students that may adversely affect the validity of test score inferences."

- AERA, APA, & NCME, 2014
Standard 12.7

I was once in a class where the teaching assistant held an optional study session for an exam. I was so glad I went to that session because some of the practice items were identical to items that appeared on the test. I am quite sure I would have gotten a worse score had I not gone. This is exactly what a study session should *not* be.

Importantly, any information disseminated to students about the exam needs to be made available to *all* students. Many classes are structured such that separate sections meet in smaller groups. In many cases, sections (or entire classes) may hold a study session specific to the exam to be administered. To ensure fair testing, be sure that all students have access to the information shared in these sections, for example, what will be covered on the test, how the grading will be performed, and how much the exam will contribute to the final grade. It is also important to be consistent about releasing practice items or questions to all students. If some students are able to prepare for the test in ways that other students are not, then this difference can introduce noise in the test scores.

Additionally, you might consider setting expectations about the specific directions of the different sections of the test. By providing students with the directions well before the exam, you give the students an equal opportunity to ask about or look up terms that might be unclear to them. This is especially helpful for non-native speakers who might need additional support understanding the language.

Test Takers' Rights to Information Prior to Testing

"Information about test content and purposes that is available to any test taker prior to testing should be available to all test takers."

- AERA, APA, & NCME, 2014
Standard 8.1

Further, set expectations about what kind of support you will provide during the test administration. For example, will you define words for students as they are taking the test? Will you allow students to look up words in a dictionary? Whatever policies you adopt, make sure you and your potential test proctors adhere to your plan and are consistent in their treatment across all students.

Set Expectations about Grading

Many centers for teaching and learning suggest that instructors inform students on how specific exams will be graded and how final course grades will be assigned. For your specific exam, you might specify how many points will be awarded and how these points will be converted to letter grades. If a curve will be in effect, you might discuss how the curve will be implemented. (For tips on grading curves and assigning letter grades to tests generally, see Chapter 9.)

As a part of finalizing test grades, I will recommend later that you eliminate bad items from your test. As a part of setting expectations, you might explain how you have the liberty to do this when you have evidence that a test item is not functioning as intended.

Other information should be communicated to students beforehand as well, such as time limits and how skipping an item, guessing, and responding incorrectly will be treated in the scoring. For essay exams, it is often recommended that scoring rubrics be distributed beforehand. If you will deduct points for misspelled words on open-ended questions or essays, explain your policy (e.g., professionals in the field need to be able to use and spell general and technical terms correctly in their professional communications to the scientific community, and therefore, you are providing training of this skill in the exam).

By defining grading procedures up front, you will prepare students on how to interpret test scores and how these scores will contribute to their overall grades.

Set Expectations about Codes of Conduct

In a study surveying 474 university students, Diekhoff et al. (1996) found that one of the strongest deterrents to cheating was students' fear of punishment. It is a good idea to decide before test time how you will handle cheating. Stating to students that cheating will be severely punished may be a good way to influence their behavior, but following through is an important step as well and should be considered in depth.

Test Takers' Responsibilities for Behavior
Throughout the Test Administration Process

"Test takers should be made aware that having someone else take the test for them, disclosing confidential test material, or engaging in any other form of cheating is unacceptable and that such behavior may result in sanctions."

- AERA, APA, & NCME, 2014
Standard 8.9

Clearly communicate before the exam what will not be allowed. For example, you might state explicitly that including answers on one's own test that have been lifted from the work of others is a legal offense and constitutes plagiarism. Bringing in notes (unless the test administration is open book and open note) gives some students an inherent advantage and compromises test validity. Circulating test items for other students constitutes copyright infringement. For that matter, any disclosure about details of the test that gives some or even all students an advantage degrades test validity and calls into question score interpretation.

If test validity is compromised, you (as the instructor) have the right to take action since it is your responsibility to provide a valid assessment of student performance.

If you will be using some techniques for detecting cheating you can inform students of this, if doing so will be beneficial to you. In some cases, for example, when using software to detect plagiarism, students need to be aware of this because they may need to run their work through specific software before it will be accepted by you for grading. In other cases, software can be applied to data after the fact to detect aberrant patterns. Students may or may not be informed of such procedures. Some instructors find it useful to mention the use of such software to students for the added benefit of deterring cheating.

Principles of Academic Integrity

"Clarify expectations for students. Defining and enforcing standards for academic integrity should be a shared undertaking with students. Nonetheless, faculty members have primary responsibility for designing the educational environment and experience. They must clarify course expectations in advance regarding honesty in academic work, including the nature and scope of student collaboration."

- McCabe and Pavela, 2004
Principle 6

Additionally, you might want to specify what will be disallowed inside the room during the test administration. Examples include possession of certain devices (such as smartphones) and clothing (such as hats and sunglasses) that may harbor inappropriate behavior such as hiding notes.

Clearly, if your class is small and the students taking the class are mature, these discussions can be tailored. Again, you are the best judge of what is appropriate for your students.

Set Expectations for Those Who Need Accommodations

The Americans with Disabilities Act (ADA) of 1990 and the ADA Amendments Act of 2008 require that colleges and universities provide reasonable accommodations for students with documented disabilities so that the offered programs and activities are fully accessible to these students. You might request that students needing special accommodations contact you privately so that you and the student can inform the appropriate campus office and determine a suitable accommodation well before an exam. At the beginning of your course, for example, outline the procedure for requesting accommodations and provide deadlines so that students are not approaching you at the last minute. Students should provide you with appropriate documentation by a qualified professional such as a physician or psychologist. The submitted documentation should be relevant to the requested accommodation. Always keep in mind that a student's disability status needs to remain confidential.

Validity of Interpretations

"Test users should inform individuals who may need accommodations in test administration about the availability of accommodations and, when required, should see that these accommodations are appropriately made available."

- AERA, APA, & NCME, 2014
Standard 9.14

An institution of higher learning needs to consider the situation on a case-by-case basis. An example of a reasonable accommodation is providing a student who has a documented learning disability with a separate room and extra time for taking an exam. Research has shown that allowing students extra time helps to eliminate disability-related decreases in scores for learning-disabled students (Huesman & Frisbie, 2000). Other common accommodations include altering the mode in which information is conveyed to the student, for example, offering the exam in Braille for a blind student, or changing the mode in which the student responds, for example, having a student with a broken wrist provide spoken responses instead of written responses. Talk with your department and university if you have questions or concerns about accommodations and their effects on the validity of your test.

Students have filed lawsuits because they have not received appropriate accommodations (Wynne v. Tufts University School of Medicine, 1991; Indiana Department Of Human Services v. Firth, 1992). Therefore, it is essential to be aware of the right to accommodations and to attend to requests promptly and appropriately.

Set Expectations about Make-Up Tests

There are many reasons why students might want a make-up exam. For example, a fire alarm might have gone off during the exam period or technical problems might have occurred during the administration of a computerized test. There are also many reasons why students might miss a test including illness, travel plans or conflicts. Instructors deal with these situations differently (for example, providing a make-up test, allowing students to drop the grade of one test, or giving extra weight to other exams). Whatever your policies are for administering make-up exams or retesting, make sure you communicate these policies in writing with students before they sit down to take the exam. There should be no surprises.

Dissemination of Information

"Test users should explain to test takers their opportunities, if any, to retake an examination ..."

- AERA, APA, & NCME, 2014
Standard 9.18

In sum, the main suggestion for preparing students for the test is to set expectations. Ask those with an accommodation request to contact you as soon as possible. Tell all students about the general content of the test, how the exam will be graded, how the test score will impact final grades, what the expected code of conduct will be, and what the policies are on retesting. If your policies are described upfront, then you set expectations for students and alleviate your need to justify decisions for every situation that arises.

CHAPTER 8:

Administering the Test

An important step in the testing process is to provide students with a fair opportunity to demonstrate what they have learned. It is the responsibility of the person administrating the test to ensure that the students all have an equal chance to do so. In testing terms, this means that everything should be standardized. According to the *Standards*, "When directions, testing conditions, and scoring follow the same detailed procedures for all test takers, the test is said to be standardized. Without such standardization, the accuracy and comparability of score interpretations would be reduced" (AERA, APA, & NCME, 2014). The only exception to this is when there is a conscious effort to make a testing opportunity equal for someone who needs accommodations, for example, for individuals with disabilities.

Standards for Fairness

"Test takers should receive comparable treatment during the test administration and scoring process."

- AERA, APA, & NCME, 2014
Standard 3.4

When the test administration is standardized, then there are no differences that might adversely influence score interpretation differentially across students, at least any that are stemming from the testing process. So, all students should receive the same directions and follow the same protocols during the exam. Even differences such as providing some students with exams printed on one side of the paper and others printed on both sides can introduce unwanted differences.

Providing a Fair Testing Environment

A fair testing environment for examinees means that everyone is treated equally during the test administration (with the exception of students who might follow different procedures due to predetermined accommodations).

A fair testing environment not only means equal test administration across students, but adequacy as well. For example, the room needs to have enough light for all students to be able to read the test comfortably. Other examples include adequate temperature control and sufficient acoustics to be able to hear the exam proctor.

I once took a standardized exam in a concert hall where the lighting was very scarce because the hall was designed for an audience to view a performance on the stage. Granted the lighting was scarce for everyone in that room, but even though we had equal treatment, it was not adequate. At the end of the day, our test scores were being compared to others who had taken the test at other facilities with sufficient lighting. Maybe the score difference in good conditions would have been similar, but I do remember squinting and rereading questions several times because of the poor lighting. I didn't bother saying anything about it, but today I would have.

Test Administration

"The testing environment should furnish reasonable comfort with minimal distractions to avoid construct-irrelevant variance."

- AERA, APA, & NCME, 2014
Standard 6.4

The issue of a fair testing environment can arise when there is not enough classroom space. Often for normal lectures, only half the students show up, but then, all of a sudden when there is an exam, all the enrolled students appear and flood the lecture hall. In the past, I have proctored exams where students were spilling over and had to use the steps for seats and books for writing surfaces. Unfortunately, this situation did not reflect a fair testing environment. If some students have access to a seat and a desk, then all students should have access to a seat and a desk.

Fairness and Computerized Equipment

There are more issues to consider if using computerized equipment or devices during the exam. For one, the students should be given the opportunity to become familiar with the equipment. If some students are familiar with a keyboard while others are not, then the test may be measuring computer skills in addition to your construct of interest. Presenting some practice items administered on the equipment would be an appropriate way to ensure that all students have a chance to become familiar with the administration modality. Additionally, the equipment should be comparable across examinees. For example computers or devices should have the same processing speed such that the experience of seeing visuals or processing algorithms is not significantly different across students. Having someone trained to deal with hardware, software, connectivity and other computer problems during the test administration will also help ensure that all students have an equal opportunity to take the test and submit answers, even when computer glitches arise.

Preventing Cheating

As the instructor, it is perfectly fine to take active steps toward ensuring that test score interpretation is not compromised because of cheating.

One technique to prevent cheating is to assign seats or situate students so that there is an empty seat between each person. Another technique is to discourage students from bringing into the testing site any clothing or technology that would assist them with inappropriate communication or information look-up.

More and more, instructors are using available technologies for detecting plagiarism or strange response patterns in tests. It is a sad reality that such technologies need to be developed and used, but we all know that cheating happens, and when it does, it invalidates the interpretation of test scores.

Test Administration

"Reasonable efforts should be made to ensure the integrity of test scores by eliminating opportunities for test takers to attain scores by fraudulent or deceptive means."

- AERA, APA, & NCME, 2014
Standard 6.6

Proctoring a Test

A common practice for discouraging cheating is to have the test proctored, that is, having physical bodies in the exam room observing students and making sure there is no funny business.

If teaching assistants or other aids are helping to proctor your exam, it is important to provide them with the appropriate training and oversight so that all students have a consistent experience taking the test. Proctors will benefit from understanding why standardized test administration is important for the validity and fairness of the test.

With proctoring, we can learn quite a bit from previous experiences of other instructors. For example, having a proctor interrupt or stop a test administration for suspected cheating may not be the most desirable, as then the burden of proving that cheating occurred is left to the proctor, with no evidence from the test itself. A different approach is to allow proctors to make observations and use this information in conjunction with other evidence. So instead of focusing on cheating, attention is placed on potential challenges to the test's validity. If the proctor claims that the test administration was not standardized for a specific reason and these observations are corroborated with patterns in the test responses, then canceling the test result is a reasonable action because evidence supports the fact that the test scores may be invalid (Semko & Hunt, 2013). In this way, courts have upheld the decision to cancel a test score, even when cheating had not been explicitly proven.

Another reason to have proctors take a more passive role is so that a proctor's actions do not affect surrounding test takers and invalidate their test scores. In the court case Mindel v. ETS, 559 N.Y.S. 2d 95 (Sup. Ct. NY 1990), a proctor suspected cheating and wanted to compare answers between the suspected cheater and a nearby test taker (the plaintiff). The proctor took the plaintiff's test booklet, causing a disruption for the plaintiff.

Again, you may want to take some time to train proctors on what to do during the test administration so that they are prepared to react in a consistent way. Spell out the process and procedures they should follow. As a part of this training, consider some of these questions: What should the proctors do when they suspect cheating? What should they do if a student asks what a question means on the test? What about an individual word? What about the directions? What should they do if they observe students talking? As a part of training, specify what actions proctors should take after these student behaviors are observed. For example, it is often recommended by test professionals that if something occurs that changes or disrupts a standard test administration, this information should be documented in writing. This way, if there are problems or challenges afterward, this documented information can be considered. It might even be the case that a change or disruption to the standard test administration is so significant that it invalidates test score interpretation for some students.

Unfortunately, many times when I was a test proctor, I was never trained on what to do. I was asked questions during a test administration, and I wasn't sure how to answer them. I am sure other proctors were fielding similar questions and probably answering these questions in different ways. Unfortunately, some test administrations were probably not standardized across students. Some simple training prior to test administration would have ameliorated this problem.

Some universities promote honor codes and codes of conduct, which include unproctored exams. The *Standards* cautions that standardized test administration cannot be ensured when tests are unproctored (p. 65). On the flip side, others go the extra mile when proctoring and even proctor in a hall outside the exam room before, during, and after the test to ensure that student behavior is in line. Ultimately, decisions need to be balanced against the rules and regulations of the university and/or department.

Offering Accommodations

As mentioned in the previous chapter, the Americans with Disabilities Act (ADA) of 1990 and the ADA Amendments Act of 2008 require that colleges and universities provide reasonable accommodations for students with documented disabilities so that their programs and activities are fully accessible to these students.

Your department and university should be able to help you implement appropriate accommodations for your students. Some examples are listed in Table 8-1.

Table 8-1. Examples of Accommodations

Challenge or Disability	Accommodation
Attention deficit (hyperactivity) disorder	Extra time, separate room
Learning disability	Extra time, separate room
Blind or visual challenges	Braille, enlarged text, text magnification, different presentation mode, reader
Deaf or hearing challenges	Sign translator
Physical challenges	Scribe, text-to-speech devices

The list above is not intended to be exhaustive but simply provides a few examples of the kinds of disabilities and cognitive, sensory, and physical challenges that might warrant test accommodations. If a student has a documented need for an accommodation, then the accommodation is required by law. To achieve fairness, appropriate accommodations make sense if they remove construct-irrelevant variance introduced by these challenges. That said, the student needs to provide the appropriate documentation well before the test administration. For this reason, it is recommended that instructors outline the procedure for requesting accommodations early in the course.

If an accommodation requires a test to be presented in a different format, for example, in Braille, then not only the items, but all the written directions and examples need to be presented in this alternate format as well. This makes sense from a fairness perspective so that all examinees are given the same instructions and examples.

A good accommodation is one that does not alter the construct being measured. For example, Huesman and Frisbie (2000) found that extended time improved test scores for learning-disabled students but this same time extension did not significantly improve scores for non-learning-disabled students. This is an ideal result. It is, however, possible that some accommodations may appear to make a test easier generally and in doing so distort test score interpretation. For example, another study showed that scores for both disabled and nondisabled groups improved (Alster, 1997). This is a tricky situation regarding the interpretation of test scores. In this case, because the improvement was *differentially* larger for the disabled group, some scholars claim that the accommodation still allowed for valid score interpretation (Fuchs & Fuchs, 2001; Sireci, Scarpati, & Li, 2005).

If you do offer accommodations, it is good practice to document each accommodation including which individuals received the accommodation, the reasons and evidence underlying the decision to offer the accommodation, the approach that was implemented and reasons why this approach was adopted, procedural notes, and any differences to scoring methods. Whatever your personal beliefs are regarding accommodations, it is useful to have reference points to support decisions made in order to comply with the law.

The main point regarding test administration is to be fair. This means offering a standardized testing protocol that is equal for all students, a fair testing environment where cheating is discouraged, and appropriate accommodations for students who qualify for them.

CHAPTER 9:

Scoring Tests and Finalizing Grades

Once students have turned in their tests, you are presented with the task of coming up with fair, final test grades. This phase of the testing process can be the most important for ensuring the validity of a test, and yet many of the procedures outlined in this chapter are often neglected. For selected-response exams, the scoring may seem like the easiest part. And yes, if all the items are functioning well, then it is just a matter of marking student answers as correct or incorrect based on a key. But more often than not, a handful of items do not function well. It is this diagnosis of item performance that will be addressed in the first part of this chapter. Next will be some tips for ensuring reliability and fairness in essay scoring. Following this, the chapter will present different approaches to providing interpretations of the test scores in the form of final test grades. Finally, the chapter concludes with other analyses that will help improve future tests.

If you have administered an essay exam, just jump to the section on scoring essays.

Screening Out Bad Items

To avoid awkward situations in which a student comes to you and argues that an item was bad (or that the test was unfair), you can preemptively invest some time understanding the functioning of your items and, if necessary, screen out bad items and adjust scores before assigning final test grades.

Screening Out Incorrect Items

Clearly, if a mistake was made in the test creation process and there exists an error in the item or answer key, the mistake needs to be addressed. Either the scoring needs to be adjusted or the item needs to be discarded. Decisions along these lines need to be made on an item-by-item basis. To be fair, if you adjust the scoring for one student, you should adjust the scoring for all students.

Screening Out Items That Are Not Sensitive to Performance *(Please Consider Doing This)*

When I was a graduate student grading tests using a scoring machine, I learned that the software we were using produced some interesting statistics about each item. For example, it could tell you what percentage of students got an answer right and what proportion of students selected each choice for each item.

Without having any formal training in Testing Theory, it was a mystery to me what this information meant at a practical level. There was one question, for example, that only 4% of the students got correct. Did this mean that this was a bad item? How could you tell if the item was a bad item or whether it was simply difficult? For another question, the majority of the students selected one of the distractors instead of the correct answer. Was this a good item? Or was the distractor just very tempting? Now, after some training, I realize that Testing Theory has the answers.

When trying to determine if an item is good or bad, the main deciding factor is the item's ability to discriminate students who have mastered the material from those students who have not. The key is to look at who is getting the item correct and who is getting it wrong. If only the high-performing students are getting the answer right, then the item is simply difficult. On the other hand, if mid- and low-performing students are also getting the answer correct or if they are the only ones getting the item correct and the high-performing students are getting it wrong, then there is something wrong with the item. With these patterns, the item is not doing what it is intended to do, and that is measure mastery of the content.

Analyzing an Item's Ability to Discriminate

So how do you figure out who is getting the item correct? One of the most accepted ways of evaluating an item is to calculate a correlation. The technical term for the kind of correlation used in item analysis is a *point-biserial*. Instead of correlating two sets of things that are on a continuous scale, you are simply correlating one thing that is on a continuous scale (test scores) and one thing that has only two possible values: correct or incorrect (items). At a high level, what you are doing is correlating a response on a single question with the student's overall test score. The overall test score is an indicator of whether the student is high-performing or low-performing. If an item is functioning well, then it will correlate with the overall test scores of your students. Often scoring software will provide this information for you. The following is a hypothetical example. Responses are coded as 1 if correct and 0 if incorrect.

Table 9-1. Example of How Responses to an Individual Item Correlate with Overall Scores

	Column A	Column B	Column C	Column D
Row 1		Response to Item 1	Response to Item 1 (Coded)	Overall Test Score
Row 2	Student 1	Correct	1	90
Row 3	Student 2	Correct	1	85
Row 4	Student 3	Correct	1	79
Row 5	Student 4	Incorrect	0	73
Row 6	Student 5	Incorrect	0	65
Row 7				
Row 8			Correlation (point-biserial) =	0.85

In this example, the students with the highest test scores are the students who answered the question correctly; whereas, the two students who did not score as well on the test got the question wrong. This is an example of a good item. Actually, this item is almost unrealistically good. You usually see point-biserials between 0.15 and 0.65.

A high point-biserial reflects the fact that the item is doing a good job of discriminating your high-performing students from your low-performing students. Values for point-biserials can range from -1.00 to 1.00. Values of 0.15 or higher mean that the item is performing well (Varma, 2006). Generally the students with high scores are answering it correctly and the students with low scores are getting it wrong. Point-biserials around zero indicate that there is no clear pattern. For example, some high-performing students may be getting the item right, but so are some low-performing students.

Point-biserials that are negative signify a big problem. With this pattern, the high-performing students are getting the answer wrong and the low- and/or mid-performing students are getting it right. This pattern is the complete opposite of what makes for a good item. Researchers have recommended removing items that have a negative point-biserial (Kaplan & Saccuzzo, 2013). Clearly, deleting half the items on your test because of negative point-biserials is not a desirable outcome, and you may decide to be a little lenient on which items you keep this time around. But awareness of item discrimination issues can help you make decisions regarding what cut-off you want to choose in the future, which will ultimately help you to improve future tests.

If your software provides the point-biserials for each item, then all you have to do is look at the number. If your software does not provide a point-biserial, the calculation can be done easily using Excel® software. See Appendix B for a detailed description. (Of course, you can also use other programs, such as R or SPSS.)

After you have identified and removed problematic items in your test, you should recalculate the scores.

A Few Notes about Difficulty

Professional test developers will also analyze items and screen out those that are too easy or too difficult. For a standardized test, where the main goal is to distinguish high-performers from low-performers, a very easy or difficult item does not serve much of a purpose because it provides no information about who is a high- versus low-performer. However, such an item might serve a purpose on a test that is specifically geared toward content mastery. It may be that you want to ensure that students master a very easy concept and so this item on the test specifically addresses this content.

You can figure out how difficult an item is simply by tallying the number of people who got the item correct and dividing this number by the total number of people who took the test. This will give you the proportion of students who got the item right. The technical term for this number is the *p-value*. Low p-values mean that the item was difficult and high p-values mean that it was easy.

Generally, professional test developers like to see items that range in difficulty from just above chance performance (for example, p-values no lower than 0.30), to just under ceiling effects (for example, p-values no higher than 0.90). A nice range of difficulties across your items ensures that your test is able to measure all along the continuum of mastery.

Because of the overhead involved in deleting items, especially from a test that has already been administered, I do not recommend vetting items based on difficulty for classroom tests.

Sometimes questions of overall test difficulty arise. Was the test too hard? Too easy? How did it compare to tests of previous years? These questions are surprisingly difficult to answer because of the many variables at play. If there is a difference, let's say, in the average overall p-value from this year's test compared to last year's test, we simply do not have enough information from our p-values to be able to determine whether it was the group of students that was different, whether the difficulty of the test was different, or whether it was a combination of these things. Even if you were to place some items from a previous test administration (for example from a previous year) in your current test, differences in item difficulty computed from p-values would not necessarily mean that the items were different. The reason for the difference might equally be due to the students. In fact, an entire field of statistical study called Item Response Theory (IRT) was developed in order to solve these problems. Although it would be ideal to create new tests of the same difficulty year after year, this feat is quite challenging. Test publishers spend a great deal of time, money, and energy creating test forms that use different items but that are the same with regard to difficulty. They do so by testing hundreds of students and by using sophisticated analyses. Unfortunately, these steps are not practical in the classroom, although not impossible by any means.

All that said, item difficulty analysis can give you ideas about which types of items were easier or more difficult for students, and this information can improve future item writing. You can compare item difficulty with your test blueprint and see if your difficulty distribution was in the ballpark. If not, you will know what kind of items to include the next time around.

Scoring Essays

In Chapter 5, scoring rubrics were discussed in detail. In this section, the focus turns to how to implement the essay scoring process.

The suggestions presented here are aimed at improving two problems observed with essay scoring: poor reliability and bias.

Improving Poor Reliability

As mentioned in Chapter 3, essay scoring can be extremely unreliable. In a study by Brimi (2011), essay scores from English teachers, who were professionally trained on an identical grading system for writing, assigned letter grades ranging from an A to an F to the same essay.

So, what can we do about reliability? First, there are two kinds reliability with regard to essay scoring. The first is intra-rater reliability (consistency of scores from the same grader) and the second is inter-rater reliability (consistency of scores across different graders). Each will be discussed in turn.

Use a Rubric

With regard to intra-rater reliability, the main suggestion is simply to use a rubric. A meta-analysis suggests that the use of a rubric can help graders be more consistent within their own grading (Jonsson & Svingby, 2007).

Double Grade

Another technique for keeping tabs on yourself is to check your own consistency in grading. You can do this by scoring 5% or so of the essays twice. If you correlate the scores from your first round of grading with scores on your second round of grading, you will see what your own reliability is. If you drop below 0.70, try to introduce more rigor in your grading and revisit the rubric.

Keeping Grades Consistent with Multiple Graders

The second kind of reliability is inter-rater reliability, which can become an issue if you have assistants helping you grade the essays. Although multiple graders will certainly help make the job of essay grading go faster, an added complexity is ensuring the scores assigned by the different graders are consistent. The quality of the individual grades is important to the validity of the test. If a test is scored unreliably, then the validity suffers.

Professionals in the testing industry have a few tricks up their sleeves for ensuring consistent grading. Some of these techniques could be applied to those working in the classroom setting. The suggestions below are provided to help you amass evidence that the test was graded fairly using valid methods.

Use Quality Graders

Although you might not have the benefit of picking and choosing your teaching assistants, you do have the power to decide who and who will not help you grade essays. The assistant should have enough experience with the course content to be able to grade competently.

If at any time during the grading process, you find that a grader's marks are wildly inconsistent or too strict or too lenient, don't be shy about offering extra training or ultimately finding another assistant to take over.

Provide Adequate Training

Make the grading instructions clear and unambiguous for your graders. Help graders become comfortable with the rubric by discussing the different levels. Walk through some sample responses and explain why you graded these responses as you did. Then, have the graders score a few responses that have already been scored by you to see if the scores are consistent. You might compile a set of responses from previous years (stripped of confidential information), and use some as training materials for your graders as they practice using the rubric. All of this takes time, but the fact is that training greatly improves consistency across graders (Davis, 2015). If possible, be available to your graders if questions arise.

Assign One Item to One Grader

You might assign one grader to a specific item and another grader to a different item. In this way, you reduce inter-grader error within the same question.

Calibrate Scores Midway

An important approach to ensuring standardized scoring across graders is to check consistency in the middle of the grading process. About one third of the way through the papers, you can check whether or not there is individual drift by throwing in a response with a known score. If scores vary significantly, then stop the grading process and help graders to become recalibrated through discussion and possibly more practice items.

Double Grade

Another way to ensure consistency is to double grade about 20% of the essays. This allows you to see where discrepancies are and reach consensus. In some approaches, a third person with authority such as the instructor considers the two grades and then makes an executive decision as to what the final grade will be. In another approach, the two graders with the different grade assignments have a discussion and reach consensus. Other times, you might simply average the two scores to reach a final score.

Test Scoring

"The quality of scoring should be monitored and documented."

- AERA, APA, & NCME, 2014
Standard 6.9

In sum, the main techniques for improving reliability in essay scoring are to use a rubric, grade some responses twice, train other graders and calibrate their scores to your scores.

Yes, We Are All Biased

No matter how self-aware we are as graders, there is a natural tendency to be biased in subjective scoring. Predisposed mindsets and personal biases can adversely affect scoring in many ways. For one, we have a tendency to want to give good students a good grade, even if their performance was mediocre. It has been shown in research that if teachers know or have been told that certain students are highly intelligent or have received good grades, then the teachers tend to score work from those students higher (even when their work does not warrant it) (Bonniol, Caverni & Noizet, 1972; Hughes, Keeling, & Tuck, 1983). As another example, research has shown that graders are significantly influenced by mechanics including grammar, spelling, and punctuation, regardless of whether or not the content of the essay is complete and accurate (Rezaei & Lovorn, 2010). And still another example is the phenomenon of essays being given higher scores when written in good handwriting (Briggs, 1970; Bull & Stevens, 1979; Chase, 1979; Markham, 1976; Marshall & Powers, 1969). The following are some suggestions for how to reduce bias in essay scoring.

Conceal Student Names

As mentioned above, if a student is known to do well either because of intelligence or previous grades, then the grader is more apt to score this student's essay higher than if the student did not have such a glowing record. To overcome this bias, one suggestion is to have the student place his or her name on a cover sheet or on the back of the exam so that scoring is blind and the student's identity does not inadvertently cause bias.

Score One Item at a Time for All Students

Scoring biases can hold true even within a single exam. Kahneman (2011) describes how on the same test, scores on a first essay can influence how the grader scores subsequent essays. To control bias in this case, Kahneman suggests grading one item across all tests before moving on to the next.

Include Mechanics in the Scoring Rubric

Unfortunately, other scoring biases stem from elements that are a direct part of the essay itself, such as poor spelling and grammar. A suggestion here is to have one dimension of the rubric address mechanics. Then the poor spelling can be treated as an independent attribute. Another bias is to score an essay lower because of poor handwriting. One hope is that by calling attention to this bias, graders can become more aware and curb the tendency to be influenced by it.

Overall, one of the most important elements of essay scoring is standardization; that is, making sure that all tests are scored in the same manner. Some ways to ensure standardization are to hide the student's name while grading, grade one question at a time, and try to focus on the attribute being graded instead of other traits such as handwriting. If you document all the conscious steps you have taken to ensure reliable and fair grading, then you continue to amass further evidence of the quality of your test.

At this point, you should have a pile of tests, each with some numeric score. The next section addresses how to map those scores to letter grades.

Mapping Scores to Letter Grades

As mentioned in Chapter 3, there are different approaches to assigning grades with two techniques appearing at the extremes: scoring based on a criterion and scoring based on a population of students. The reality is that most scoring in the classroom will fall somewhere in the middle. Most instructors start with criterion scoring and then make some adjustments based on group performance. There is no right or wrong way, and surveys have shown there is quite a bit of variation among teachers (Waltman & Frisbie, 1994). By understanding the range of possible approaches to assigning grades, you can articulate to students your approach and your reasons behind it.

Scoring Based on a Criterion

One approach to assigning grades is to embrace the idea that students must master a certain amount of material to earn a given grade and that the performance of the class as a whole has absolutely no bearing on the grades whatsoever. According to this approach, there is a standard, or a criterion, that needs to be met that is independent of the test taking population. All students could get As; and likewise, all students could get Fs. The canonical assignment for the criterion-referenced approach is by percentage of content mastered according to the following:

A = 90%-100%

B = 80%-89%

C = 70%-79%

D = 60%-69%

F = 0%-59%

The advantage of this approach is that clear guidelines can be defined beforehand of what is expected in order to receive an A, B, C, D, and F. Also, students perceive criterion-referenced grading as fair (Dalbert, Schneidewind, & Saalbach, 2007). The downside is that a test's difficulty might drift from year to year, so what one student was required to answer correctly in Year X might have been easier than what another student in Year Y had to answer correctly.

A variation to this approach is to go through your exam to decide on the criterion level for each grade. With the canonical cut point 90 for the A cut, the assumption is that someone who receives an A should understand and respond correctly to 90% of the content on the test. Alternatively, you could go through the test and for each question, decide whether or not an A- student would get that item correct. Then count the number of points an A-student would be expected to score on the test as a whole and set that score as the A/B cut point. This process then needs to be repeated for all cut points.

Scoring Based on the Group

Another approach is to base grades on the performance of a group of students. Usually in professional testing, a large sample of students is tested that represents the target population (called the norming sample) and performances from this sample are used to give some meaning to a score. For example, the score 550 might not mean much in isolation, but if you also add the fact that the score was in the 70th percentile, then you know that it was not the best score but was solidly above average. Usually, a norming sample is comprised of a very large number of students so the distribution of observed scores often takes the shape of a bell curve. This is the case for intelligence tests. If you were to give 1000 people an intelligence test, the most frequent score would be 100. About 70% of the group would score between 85 and 115. About 2.5% would score at the very low end of the scale (below 70) and about 2.5% would score at the very high end of the scale (above 130). An amazing number of things we measure related to human beings is distributed like a bell-shaped curve.

Now, in the classroom, there are no norming samples aside from the group of students who took the test. So, often if this approach is adopted, then it is the test-taking students who are serving as the norming population. Basically, what is happening is that you are grading students based on their relative performance to other students.

Depending on the cohort of students in the class, assigning grades solely based on the test-taking student population can be beneficial or detrimental to a student's grade. If all the students bombed a test, then this style of grading can significantly boost grades for a failing student. In contrast to this, good performances can result in bad grades if other students' performances are stronger. This is often seen in some law and business schools. In one classroom, a student's grade of an A minus was converted to a C. Unfortunately, as a reaction to this, the student filed a lawsuit against the university, claiming that his civil rights and contractual rights were violated (Saltzman, 2007). The plaintiff did not win the case, but it is good to know that this style of grading can produce some disgruntled students.

Some see group-referenced scoring as beneficial because it controls for grade inflation and induces healthy competition among students. However, others see it as a disadvantage because from a grader's perspective there is less of a direct link between the student's performance and the grade. Researchers have noted that this style of grading has been associated with very negative grading experiences (Guskey, 2006). Also, not all observed scores from a test result in a pretty bell-shaped curve. Many test score distributions are skewed. In these cases, it could be argued that percentages based on a theoretical bell curve should not be forced onto distributions of other shapes.

So how do you actually translate the bell curve into grades? The bell curve is also referred to as the normal distribution, which has been studied extensively. We know that most people will fall within three standard deviations of the middle (either above or below). We also know, for every point in the distribution, what the percentage of students performing better or worse at that given point is. Taking these two pieces of information together, one technique is to divide the bell curve into grades using standard deviations like the following:

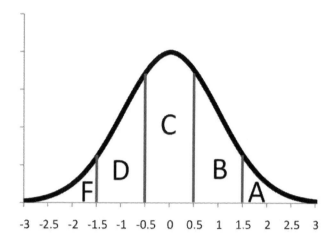

Figure 9-2. Example of grade cut points based on standard deviations of the normal distribution.

After you place the cut points, then the percentage of students at these points in the distribution can be used to assign the grades. We know that at 1.5 standard deviations above the mean, the percent of students at that point and higher is about 7%. We can look up the percent for each cut point and get the following:

Top 7% = As

Next 24% = Bs

Middle 38% = Cs

Lower 24% = Ds

Lowest 7% = Fs

Then you simply rank your students according to their test scores. Using these rankings, figure out the top-most 7% (most likely, you'll come close but not hit 7% exactly because you will want to include everyone who got a given grade). Then assign these folks an A. For Bs, take the next 24%. For Cs, find the next 38%. Then for the next 24%, assign Ds. Finally, give the remaining 7% of the students Fs.

Other people divide the curve differently such that one standard deviation above and below the mean is a C. This results in the following breakdown:

Top 2.5% = As

Next 13.5% = Bs

Middle 68% = Cs

Lower 13.5% = Ds

Lowest 2.5% = Fs

Still others shift the assignment so that more As and Bs are assigned than Ds and Fs (Wedell, Parducci & Roman, 1989):

Top 15% = As

Next 25% = Bs

Middle 45% = Cs

Lower 10% = Ds

Lowest 5% = Fs

More lenient cut points are common. Some researchers have found that the average grade assigned by most teachers is a B- (not a C) (Waltman & Frisbie, 1994).

As you can see, the slicing and dicing can be somewhat arbitrary, so whichever decision you make, it might be best to be able to back it up with a reasonable argument.

Both criterion-referenced and group-referenced approaches to assigning grades have their merits, but the reality is that most instructors will choose a solution somewhere in the middle. The next section addresses some of these techniques in between criterion-referenced and group-referenced grading.

Grading with Both Approaches

For most instructors, final grades on a test will be based on the actual scores from the test with some kind of adjustment related to how the group of students performed. This approach is more comfortable for many instructors who do not want to fail an entire group of students. And personally, I have benefited from it. When I was an undergraduate, all the students across all calculus classes were required to take the same test written by a central committee. I failed the test in the sense that I answered only a few questions correctly. Feeling depressed about my performance, I was amazed to find that all the students in my class had failed the test as well (this was back in the day when grades were simply posted on doors). I was relieved to discover that I had received an A because I had performed relatively better than the rest of the other failing students (I hope that the school has since selected another instructor to teach the class).

Adjusting test scores is actually seen as fair by students because most take this approach when asked to assign grades themselves. In a research study by Wedell, Parducci, and Roman (1989), students were presented with four sets of test scores and were asked to mark where they felt cut points should be for assigning traditional grades (A, B, C, D, and F). Most students took a hybrid approach where they paid attention to the range of scores (as in a criterion-referenced approach), but then also considered the frequency of students scoring within that range (as in the group-referenced approached).

So, how do you make adjustments to the scores? The following are four approaches.

Placing Cut Points at Scoring Gaps

One technique for adjusting grades based on group performance is to place the cuts at scoring gaps. Consider a 100-point test where some students received 91s, 90s, 89s, and 87s. Since nobody got an 88, this score would be an ideal cut point for an A-. This approach makes sense because, even in the professional testing realm, there is always a discussion of how much error there is surrounding a cut point. What is to say that the step from 89% to 90% is the exact point at which someone receives a B versus an A? When there is a gap in the score distribution, then there is less confrontation because none of the students would have just missed the traditional cut-off point.

Shifting the Average Score

Another approach for adjusting grades is to shift the average score. To do this, first find the average score of all the tests and compare this to your ideal average score. The difference will be the amount you shift all scores. Assign grades based on the student's score plus or minus this shift (basing grades on the canonical 90%-100% = As, 80%-89% = Bs, etc.) An even better statistic to use is the median (rank all the grades and find the middle one). A median will give you a better picture of what the middle score is when the distribution is skewed.

Shifting the Highest Score

Another common approach is to take the highest grade on the test and calculate the difference between this score and 100%. Then shift all test scores this amount. Although easy to do, this approach is less robust to outliers (cases when you have one brilliant student compared to the rest of the class).

Adjusting the Number of Points

Yet another approach to adjusting grades (usually to boost scores) is to reduce the number of points possible. An example is to use the following equation:

$$\text{Number of points possible} = \frac{\text{Average score}}{\text{Ideal Average \% (e.g., 75\% or 0.75)}}$$

Often this will push high scores into percentages above 100%, but you may not mind this (and I'm sure the select students won't mind).

The above list of methods for mapping scores to letter grades is, of course, not exhaustive. Instructors are always devising new ways of assigning grades. What this section has provided is an overview of different approaches to help you decide where you fall on the spectrum of criterion- versus group-referenced grading and give you some tools that you can apply in your own classroom. At the end of the day, the grading assignment approach you choose will be determined by your personal grading philosophy coupled with policy guidelines from your institution. Importantly, whatever approach you take, advertise it to students before the test and back it up where you can with solid logic.

Analyzing Your Test to Improve Future Tests

Checking Reliability

At this point in the process, you might consider understanding your test's reliability level. Obviously, you cannot improve the reliability for the test you just administered, but knowing what the reliability is can help you predict reliability on future tests with different numbers of items. Once you have done this calculation a few times, you will have a good idea of how many questions you will need the next time around. In addition, if you perform this calculation, you will have documented evidence of the reliability of your test, which will help you stand behind your grading.

Standards for Reliability/Precision

"Appropriate evidence of reliability/precision should be provided for the interpretation for each intended score use."

- AERA, APA, & NCME, 2014
Standard 2.0

There are different ways to estimate reliability. One of the easiest is to measure consistency within a test. This is called internal reliability. A simple way to compute internal reliability is to use a split-half technique. Appendix A has a description of how to do this with Excel® software.

Interpreting Reliability Results

Reliability coefficients can range from 0.00 to 1.00. The closer the reliability coefficient is to one, the better your reliability. Some claim that internal reliability should not fall below 0.70 (Kline, 2000). If your reliability is 0.70 or above, then this means there are enough items in your test. Reliabilities in the range of 0.60 to 0.69 are okay. The reliability is not great, but some would consider this fine for a classroom test. If you are motivated to improve the reliability, consider adding more items next time. If the reliability is below 0.60, then you owe it to your students to increase the reliability next time. Other sources raise a flag at a reliability of 0.50 (Vegada, Karelia & Pillai, 2014).

Checking Distractors

Another analysis to consider is checking your distractors. The purpose of this step is to help you create future items by allowing you to reuse distractors that were effective and avoid those that did not do their jobs. The role of the distractor is to do just what its name suggests: distract. Ideally, low-performing students are tempted by these choices.

A simple way of analyzing distractors is to generate a tally of the number of students who selected the distractor and divide by the total number of students who took the test. This is the proportion of students who selected the distractor. If this number is less than 0.02, then the distractor was not appealing. Distractors with high numbers are candidates for use in future items with similar content.

A more sophisticated way to analyze distractors is to determine what the correlation was between selecting the distractor and the student's total score. This technique is similar to calculating the item's point-biserial (described in Appendix B). You are doing the same thing, but instead of correlating the correct answer with the total score, you are correlating each distractor with the total score. This time you will be looking for negative numbers. The more negative the better. The reasoning here is that if high-achievers are selecting the distractors (and pushing the correlation in the positive direction), then the distractor is actually a viable option for those students who should know better. If the correlation is very negative, then the low-performing students tend to be the ones selecting the distractor, which is desirable.

Keep these results for later and resurface them when it is item writing time again.

This chapter covered important material for scoring your test and finalizing grades. First was a discussion of how to screen out bad items that are not sensitive to high versus low performance. This important step of using point-biserials in item analysis can greatly enhance the validity evidence of any test. Then, some tips were presented on how to score essays reliably. The next topic was how to map scores to letter grades. The basics of criterion-referenced scoring were compared to group-referenced scoring and some tips were provided for those who fall somewhere in the middle of these extremes (for example, placing cut points at gaps or shifting the average score). Finally, some analyses were presented that can help development of future tests such as how to calculate test reliability and how to determine if distractors are working. From here, there is only one more step to go, and that is returning the tests.

CHAPTER 10:

Reporting Grades and Returning Tests

This chapter covers details about reporting grades and returning tests, including suggestions for how to handle suspected cheating and challenged grades. Many issues discussed are a matter of opinion, but we can still draw upon guidelines provided by standards bodies and other professionals in the field.

Notifying Students of When to Expect Graded Tests

Standards bodies agree that students have a right to receive scores from their tests within a reasonable amount of time after taking the test. Generally, scores that are returned sooner rather than later provide students with the best learning experience because immediate feedback is assimilated better than feedback provided after a delay (Epstein et al., 2002).

If there will be significant delays in returning tests for any reason, notify students of the delays and if possible provide them with a reasonable date that the scores will be available.

Dissemination of Information

"Unless circumstances clearly require that test results be withheld, a test user is obligated to provide a timely report of the results to the test taker and others entitled to receive this information."

- AERA, APA, & NCME, 2014
Standard 9.16

Providing Context for the Test Scores

Test scores are really just numbers, and without any context, this number is difficult to interpret. However, in most academic environments, test scores will be presented in terms of percent correct (usually out of 100%) and/or in term of grades A, B, C, D, and F, which are common and easily interpretable by students (I got an A, so I aced it; versus I got an F so I failed it.) Sometimes, additional information such as what the average score was on the test can help students interpret their performance in comparison to others in the class.

Protecting the Confidentiality and Security of Student Information

Regardless of the type of information you return to the student, it is vital that each student's personally identifiable information remain confidential and secure. This means that no one other than the student should be able to gain access to the scores and that the student's information should remain protected from exposure. The grades should also be kept secure to avoid unintended modification or loss.

Reporting and Interpretation

"Transmission of individually identified test scores to authorized individuals or institutions should be done in a manner that protects the confidential nature of the scores and pertinent ancillary information."

- AERA, APA, & NCME, 2014
Standard 6.16

In today's age, where most everything is recorded and stored digitally, students have a right to have their test data protected electronically. Some suggestions are to use passwords and encryption when transmitting data files. For example, if a teaching assistant is emailing you a file with a list of student grades, this data transmission is actually not secure. Some applications provide ways to encrypt files to protect students' confidential information.

Another suggestion is to modify privacy settings by limiting access to folders where files of student grades are kept. Still another suggestion posed by the *Standards*, is to dissociate common personally identifying information with the grades (clearly Social Security Numbers would not meet this criterion). Instead grades can be associated with a different arbitrary label, number or code that can only be linked back to the student by a mapping file stored in a different place.

In general, federal law prohibits the release of grades to anyone other than the student. This policy originated from the Family Educational Rights and Privacy Act (FERPA), also known as the Buckley Amendment, which was put into place to protect the privacy of student education records.

Gone are the days of setting graded exams outside an instructor's office to be collected by the student. Exams need to be returned directly to the student. Also gone are the days of posting grades outside of offices using identifiable information associated with the student (including Social Security Numbers).

Even universities in the UK are starting to follow suit. It used to be a centuries-old tradition that end-of-year results were publically displayed and even published in results lists. Now universities including Oxford and Cambridge are starting to change these traditions in favor of privacy protection.

In the US, laws even prohibit the release of grades to parents. There are exceptions though. For example, the student can give consent to disclose academic information to parents, or parents might have the legal right to this information if the student is claimed as a dependent. Check with your institution's policies if the issue arises.

When During a Class to Return Tests

There are different opinions about when to return graded tests. Many instructors return them at the end of class to reduce complaints. Others return them at the beginning of class and invite discussion. Importantly, you have done your homework at this point so you can address questions with confidence.

Howard Aldrich (2001) wrote a nice paper about his approach to returning tests. Instead of placing the focus on the instructor's grading, he shifts attention to student performance and learning. First, he returns the tests at the beginning of class and plans to spend most of that class discussing it. (He writes all new questions for each exam so he feels comfortable returning the exam to students.) Then, he has students meet in groups to discuss reasons for correct answers. This step is important for taking the focus off of him as the grader and onto student performance. Finally, as motivation, he tells students that he will be giving them a short quiz based on the questions from the test that most people missed. He also makes the final exam cumulative so that students are again motivated to understand what they missed and why.

Every instructor will have a different approach. Again, the important thing to remember is that if you have followed the steps in this book, you will have a defensible test and can look to student discussions with alacrity instead of dread.

How Long to Hold Onto Student Grades and Records

Sometimes grades will be disputed. For this reason, it is useful to retain records, even after the course has ended. On the other hand, student information needs to be kept secure, so it is a liability to keep it around. As a happy middle ground, some institutions suggest holding onto graded work for one year after the course.

Dealing with Cheating

Unfortunately, instructors and teaching assistants often have to deal with a dark side of human nature – cheating. This is an uncomfortable situation, but hopefully, the information in this chapter can help lessen the anxiety posed by this unavoidable situation.

As mentioned in several previous chapters, it is a sad truth that college students are no strangers to cheating (Diekhoff et al., 1996; Gardner et al., 1988; McCabe, 1992). Even when steps have been taken to prevent cheating such as proctoring exams and explicitly telling students that inappropriate behavior will have consequences, cheating happens.

Unfortunately, it is common for instructors who notice cheating to look away. In 2002-2003, McCabe and Pavela (2004) conducted a survey with over 2,500 instructors and found that 44% had suspected cheating on at least one occasion and had chosen to ignore it. McCabe and Pavela claim that instructors send a message when reacting to challenging situations. Ignoring a problem of academic dishonesty sends a negative message that integrity is not a core value that is worth enforcing. The message from professional organizations is the same. If misconduct is suspected, then action needs to be taken. The *Standards* states that "any form of cheating or behavior that reduces the validity and fairness of the interpretations of test results should be investigated promptly with appropriate action taken." The bottom line is that action is necessary.

When investigating misconduct, the more evidence, the better. This is certainly the case when issues of cheating hit the courtroom. Courts encourage thorough investigations and want as much evidence as possible. For example, in Langston v. ACT, 890 F2d 380 (11th Cir. 1989), ACT thoroughly investigated test responses, other students' test responses, and additional information such as the student's grades from other classes.

Investigating a Student's Responses

To investigate the student's scores, you can compare expected patterns with violations of these patterns. The assumption in testing is that students generally will get easier items correct and harder items incorrect. You have information about each item's difficulty from scoring the test for the entire class. The following is a way to analyze student test responses for selected-response tests.

Arrange the data as in the example below, with the students in columns and the items in rows.

Table 10-1. Example Test Response Data Used for Suspected Cheating

	Column A	Column B	Column C	Column D
Row 1		Student 1	Student 1 (Coded)	Overall Correct Responses to Item
Row 2	Item 1	Correct	1	180
Row 3	Item 2	Correct	0	170
Row 4	Item 3	Correct	1	158
Row 5	Item 4	Incorrect	0	146
Row 6	Item 5	Incorrect	1	121
Row 7				
Row 8	Correlation		-0.12	

To generate the correlation value in cell C8, type the following:

=correl(C2:C6,D2:D6)

If the correlation is negative, then this is evidence that the student responses were showing a different pattern than those of the rest of the other students in the class.

Another thing to check is responses to difficult items. Chapter 9 described how to compute item difficulty for each item. Now, you can group the items into categories such as Very Easy, Easy, Medium, Difficult, and Very Difficult. In general, you should observe a decline in the number of items answered correctly in each of these groups if progressing from Very Easy to Very Difficult. If the pattern is lumpy or the student is getting many more Difficult or Very Difficult items correct than expected, this is evidence that the test scores cannot be confidently interpreted. Again, you may not have caught the person cheating, but if standard assumptions are violated, then you can still call the test scores into question and request a retest or take other appropriate actions.

Comparing Responses with Surrounding Students

If information is available, you could also analyze the responses of nearby students to determine if there are patterns that might suggest copying or other forms of cheating. As mentioned previously, this should be done after the exams are turned in and not during the test administration so as not to disturb other students taking the test.

Getting Student Input Regarding the Cheating Incident

The *Standards* suggests that students be given an opportunity to appeal a decision with evidence of their own. Consult established policies that need to be followed by your institution. For example, students might have the right to be represented by legal counsel.

The Final Verdict

Evidence of cheating should be made available to the student so that the student knows that an accusation is warranted. In some cases, you may not want to provide too much information, for example releasing specific items and answers to the student, because too much information might facilitate more cheating. But students should be provided with enough information so that they are made aware that there is evidence supporting a final decision.

Consequences of Cheating

The actions taken for misconduct can vary. If there is enough evidence of misconduct, a common approach is to have the instructor assign a 0 for the test. In other situations, instructors allow a retest, but this may give the student an unfair advantage if the same items are used – at this point, the student has already seen the material on the test and knows exactly what to study. If all new items are used, then this is a possible solution, as long as the content coverage and difficulty of the new items matches the original test.

Dealing with Challenged Grades

Another situation familiar to instructors is when a student disputes a grade. Often students complain about a test simply to secure the best possible grade in a class. And for many students, educational opportunities and jobs are on the line. They are intrinsically motivated, so a little pestering is a small price to pay for being granted admission to a competitive grad school or landing a coveted internship. Other students may complain because, frankly, whether we admit it or not, it is human nature to blame outside forces (you, the instructor) for an individual's poor performance. And occasionally, challenged grades can be justified. The following are some examples of legitimate complaints:

- There are multiple correct answers to a question.

- An item was ambiguous and/or unclear.

- The material covered on the test was not representative of the content covered in class.

- The material in the item was biased.

- The essay scoring was too subjective.

Hopefully, by following the guidelines in this book, many of the above complaints can be minimized.

Regardless of why the student is disputing the grade, the student has the right to fair treatment, and a process should be followed to reach resolution. Some instructors ask the complaining students to write formal descriptions of the problems and support their perspectives with evidence and details from the class notes or text. Such a process ensures that reactions to the test are well thought through by the student.

Let's go through some common complaints and discuss some options for handling them.

Scoring Errors

There may be some situations where an item was legitimately scored incorrectly. Of course, such errors should be corrected as soon as possible. The implication of this is that if the item is rescored for one student, then the item needs to be rescored for all tests. This process is time consuming, but it ensures standardized scoring.

Correct Answers That Were Not Considered

You might have a student come to you with an answer that did not appear on the key but when explained in the right light, could be considered correct. Again, if you decide to give the complaining student credit, then really you should rescore all tests so that scoring is the same and is standardized across all students.

Complaints of Tests or Items Not Representing Course Content

A common complaint is that the test was unfair because it did not align with what was covered in class. You can explain the concept of content validity to the student and show the student your test blueprint as evidence that the test has a representative number of items on the test covering intended topics of importance to mastery in the course. Then you can make reference to content covered in lectures and in the text. If applicable, explain that some items are intended to measure higher-level thinking, which is expected in the class.

Complaints of Ambiguous or Unclear Items

Hopefully, all ambiguous and/or unclear items will have been removed as a result of your review (Chapter 6) or item analysis (Chapter 9). You can show the student your test blueprint and discuss how the item is relevant to the content of the course. If appropriate, you can explain how the item is functioning well because of its ability to discriminate high-performing students from low-performing students.

Complaints of Biased Items

Again, the hope is that your careful review will have eliminated any items with potential bias. If complaints still exist, you can potentially analyze the item by seeing if there are differences across performances of select subgroups.

In all cases, make note of such complaints so that you can screen out similar items in the future.

Complaints of Essay Scoring

Some student may complain that essay scoring was too subjective. Providing a rubric and showing exemplars at the given levels and why the student's paper was assigned a specific level can help. A good defense against complaints of essay scoring is documentation of how scoring was standardized.

Another source of discontent might be when multiple graders are grading the same test. When graders are not calibrated to each other, then there may be differences in scores because of differences in graders' interpretations, not anything that has to do with the student responses. When errors of this nature are introduced, then students have a legitimate reason to complain about grades. Documentation showing how graders were calibrated with each other can provide students with evidence of standardized scoring procedures.

The Test in the Larger Context of Course Grades

According to the *Standards*, a person making decisions about a student should base these decisions on data from more than one appropriate measurement instrument. The test that you administer in your class is one of these assessment instruments, but the general guidelines suggest that there should be others. More measures of your students' abilities, knowledge, and content mastery will enhance the precision of your students' overall grades. With more measurements, you get a more consistent picture of what that student can do aside from one or two days where the student simply might have been off.

Centers of teaching and learning at universities encourage instructors to consider enough elements to ensure that a final grade has a high degree of precision (Center for Innovation in Teaching & Learning, 2016).

Use and Interpretation of Educational Assessments

"In educational settings, a decision or characterization that will have major impact on a student should take into consideration not just scores from a single test but other relevant information."

- AERA, APA, & NCME, 2014
Standard 12.10

The main points of this chapter are to keep student information confidential, to take action when cheating is suspected, and to respectfully listen to arguments about challenged grades but not to be shy about presenting evidence to the contrary.

Conclusion

Throughout this book, you have learned how to create and score a quality exam with supporting evidence of validity, reliability and fairness. In order to be valid, the test needs to cover relevant material. By creating a test blueprint with a definition of the construct and the content you specify as being important for domain mastery (and writing items in accordance with this blueprint), you provide evidence of the test's construct and content validity. By including a sufficient number of items and estimating internal reliability, you have documented evidence of the test's reliability. By writing items that avoid construct-irrelevant variance, copiously reviewing your items for potential bias, keeping the language simple, providing a standardized test administration, and offering appropriate accommodations, you ensure that your test is fair. Along the way, you have delved into research on what patterns to avoid in item writing and what analyses to run to ensure that your items are functioning properly.

Congratulations! Now remember that no measurement instrument will be perfect. But if you follow the guidelines set forth in this book, you can rest assured that your test will be abiding by professional standards and will be a sound measurement instrument that you can stand behind with confidence.

APPENDIX A:

How to Compute a Split-Half Reliability

To calculate split-half reliability, you will be tallying a subscore for all the odd items of the test and a subscore for all the even items; then you will be correlating the two subscores across all test takers. Why do an even/odd comparison instead of a first/last half comparison? You have to make sure that the halves you are comparing are comparable in style and content. The first half might be easier or might consist of different tasks compared to the second half.

Here is how to compute a split-half reliability using Excel® software.

Step 1. List your students across the top and their scored responses down the rows (0 for incorrect, 1 for correct). Then tally the values for the even-numbered items. To do this, go to a cell below Student 1's responses and type the following:

=SUM(

Then click on the Item 2 cell for Student 1 (cell B3). Then enter "+." Then click on the Item 4 cell for Student 1. Then enter "+." Continue until all the even items are entered into the formula. Finally, type a closed parenthesis ")." The formula for a 20-item test arranged as they are in Figure A-1 would be the following:

=SUM(B3+B5+B7+B9+B11+B13+B15+B17+B19+B21)

	A	B	C	D	E	F	G	H	I	J	K	L
1		Student1	Student2	Student3	Student4	Student5	Student6	Student7	Student8	Student9	Student10	
2	Item1	1	0	1	1	1	1	1	1	1	1	
3	Item2	1	0	0	1	1	1	1	1	1	1	
4	Item3	1	0	1	1	1	1	1	1	1	0	
5	Item4	1	0	1	1	1	1	1	1	1	1	
6	Item5	1	0	0	1	1	1	1	1	1	1	
7	Item6	0	0	1	1	1	1	1	1	1	0	
8	Item7	1	0	1	1	1	1	1	1	1	1	
9	Item8	0	1	0	1	1	1	1	1	1	0	
10	Item9	1	1	1	0	1	1	1	0	1	0	
11	Item10	1	0	1	1	1	1	1	1	1	1	
12	Item11	1	0	0	0	0	1	0	1	0	0	
13	Item12	0	1	1	0	0	1	1	1	1	0	
14	Item13	1	0	0	0	0	1	1	1	1	0	
15	Item14	1	0	1	1	0	1	1	1	1	1	
16	Item15	1	0	0	1	1	1	1	0	1	1	
17	Item16	1	0	0	1	0	1	1	1	1	1	
18	Item17	1	0	0	1	0	1	1	1	1	1	
19	Item18	1	0	0	1	1	1	1	1	1	1	
20	Item19	1	0	0	0	0	1	1	0	1	1	
21	Item20	1	0	0	0	0	1	0	0	1	0	
22												
23	Even subtotal	7	2	5	8	6	10	9	9	10	6	
24	Odd subtotal	10	1	4	6	6	10	9	7	9	6	
25												

Used with permission from Microsoft.

Figure A-1. Example of data layout for computing split-half reliability.

The above spreadsheet is available from the following website:
http://www.intelliphonics.com/source/resources.html.

If you are comfortable with Excel® software and come up with a more efficient way to do this step, then go for it! (For example, in a separate column you could place an E next to all the even-numbered items and an O next to all the odd-numbered items and then sort. This will allow you to select the cells you want to sum more easily.)

Step 2. Now, calculate the subtotal of the items with an odd question number. Go through the same process but select the cells with the odd items. For a test with 20 items, the formula would look like this:

=SUM(B2+B4+B6+B8+B10+B12+B14+B16+B18+B20)

Note: if you have a different number of items or a different layout, your formula will look different.

Step 3. Now compute the subtotals for the rest of the students. To do this, select the two formula cells for Student1 containing the Even subtotal and Odd subtotal. You should see a dark box around these selected cells. There is a dark square at the bottom right corner of the box as shown in Figure A-2.

Used with permission from Microsoft.

Figure A-2. Example of a dark box.

Place the cursor over this box and it should become a "+." Then click and drag to your right until you have selected cells under every student column. Once you release the mouse button, the software will automatically compute the subtotals for all your students.

Step 4. Finally, you are ready to compute the split-half reliability. The reliability is simply a Pearson correlation (technically called a Pearson Product Moment Correlation Coefficient), and the formula is a part of the Excel® software. Just type in the following:

=correl(

Then select the cells of the even subtotals. Enter ",". Then select the cells of the odd subtotals. Finally, type a closed parenthesis. For the data in Figure A-1, the resulting formula will look like this:

=correl(B23:K23,B24:K24)

Click Enter and a number will appear in the cell. This number should be between 0.00 and 1.00. This number is almost your reliability. It just needs a little adjustment.

Step 5. Why does the number need to be adjusted? It is underestimating your reliability because it is assuming that the test is half as long as it really is. To adjust it, go to the cell below and enter the following (this assumes that the Pearson formula is in cell B26):

=(2*B26)/(1+B26)

Now you have a corrected split-half reliability value.

What you just did was apply the Spearman-Brown Prophecy Formula (Brown, 1910; Spearman, 1910) to the original reliability estimate. This formula is commonly used to adjust reliability estimates when using the split-half approach.

APPENDIX B:

How to Calculate a Point-biserial

First, arrange your data into columns like the example below, with one student per row and one item per column.

Table B-1. Example Test Response Data Used for Calculating Point-Biserials.

	Col A	Col B	Col C	Col D	Col E	...	Col X
Row 1		Item 1	Item 2	Item 1 Coded	Item 2 Coded	...	Test Score
Row 2	Student 1	Correct	Correct	1	1	...	90
Row 3	Student 2	Correct	Incorrect	1	0	...	85
Row 4	Student 3	Correct	Correct	1	1	...	79
Row 5	Student 4	Incorrect	Incorrect	0	0	...	73
Row 6	Student 5	Incorrect	Correct	0	1	...	65
Row 7							
Row 8	Correlation (point-biserial) =			0.87	-0.06	...	

This spreadsheet is available online at http://www.intelliphonics.com/source/resources.html.

If your data are arranged in the opposite orientation such that the items are in the rows, a similar computation can be done (see below).

To generate the correlation value in cell D8 (the shaded cell), type the following:

=correl(D2:D6,$X2:$X6)

You will most likely have more students, so change the row numbers to include all students (for example, D6 might become D25 and $X6 might become $X25). Just make sure that the information for each individual student is represented in a single row.

Then copy the formula into each column that has item responses.

Here is what the formula means (for those who care to know):

=correl	Calculate a correlation
(…)	Using the data in the parentheses
D2:D6	Use the item scores in cells D2 through D6 (so D2, D3, D4, D5, and D6)
,	And correlate them with
$X2:$X6	The test scores in cells X2 to X6.

Why the $? Well, if you copy and paste the formula into the next cell (E8), then the column numbers will automatically change. From one perspective, this is a good thing: You will now do the calculation for the responses to Item 2 in the next column (D changes to E). But from another perspective, this is not a good thing because if X changes to Y, you will no longer be correlating the item responses with the test scores. The $ indicates that if you cut and paste the formula, it should stick with Column X. This way, the correlations will always be comparing item responses with the overall test scores in Column X.

Quickly Repeat for Each Item

A quick shortcut for copying and pasting formulae is to drag the information across cells. To do this, select cell D8. The cell should be outlined in black with a small black square in the bottom right-hand corner.

Used with permission from Microsoft.

Figure B-2. Example of dragging to the right.

Click that little square and drag your cursor to the right for the number of items in your test.

If your table is transposed, you can use the same formula, just change the cell ranges of the data as in the following example.

Table B-3. Example Test Response Data Used for Calculating Point-Biserials (Transposed).

	Col A	Col B	Col C	Col D	Col E	Col F	Col G	Col H
Row 1		S 1	S 2	S 3	S 4	S 5		Correlation (point-biserial) =
Row 2	Response to Item 1 (Coded)	1	1	1	0	0		0.87
Row 3	Response to Item 2 (Coded)	1	0	1	0	1		-0.06
Row 4	...	...	...	...	...	...		...
Row 5	Overall Test Score	90	85	79	73	65		

With this orientation, type the following in cell H2:

=correl(B2:F2,B$5:F$5)

Voila! You will see a point-biserial.

Acknowledgements

First and foremost, I would like to thank Debajit Ghosh for his love, inspiration, and support. I thank Jared Bernstein for introducing me to the field and for his many years of mentorship. I would also like to thank Carrie Armel, Cindy Donaldson, Carrie Grey, Lisa Reeves, Jennifer Ripley, and Jeff Shrager for their thoughtful ideas. Also, I would like to acknowledge my son's love and patience as I complete this multi-year project.

References

Albanese, M. A., Kent, T. H., & Whitney, D. R. (1979). Cluing in multiple choice test items with combinations of correct responses. *Journal of Medical Education, 54,* 948-950.

Albanese, M. A. & Sabers, D. L. (1978). Multiple response vs. multiple true false scoring: A comparison of reliability and validity. Paper presented at the *Meeting of the National Council on Measurement in Education,* Toronto, Canada.

Aldrich, H. (2001). How to hand exams back to your class. *College Teaching, 49*(3), 82.

Alster, E. H. (1997). The effects of extended time on algebra test scores for college students with and without learning disabilities. *Journal of Learning Disabilities, 30*(2), 222-227.

American Educational Research Association, American Psychological Association, National Council on Measurement in Education. (2014*). Standards for educational and psychological testing.* Washington, DC: American Educational Research Association.

Anastasi, A. & Urbina, S. (1997). *Psychology testing.* New York: Pearson.

Anderson, J. R. (1990). *Cognitive psychology and its implications* (p. 280-284). New York: W.H. Freeman and Company.

Anderson, L. W. & Krathwohl, D. R. (Eds.). (2001). *A taxonomy for learning, teaching, and assessing: A revision of Bloom's taxonomy of educational objectives.* New York, NY: Longman.

Anderson, L. W., Krathwohl, D. R., Airasian, P. W., Cruikshank, K. A., Mayer, R. E., Pintrich, P. R., Raths, J., & Wittrock, M. C. (2001). *A taxonomy for learning, teaching, and assessing: A revision of Bloom's taxonomy of educational objectives.* White Plains, NY: Longman.

Attali, Y. & Bar-Hillel, M. (2003). Guess where: The position of correct answers in multiple choice test items as a psychometric variable. *Journal of Educational Measurement, 40*(2), 109-128.

Baghaei, P. & Amrahi, N. (2011). The effects of the number of options on the psychometric characteristics of multiple choice items. *Psychological Test and Assessment Modeling, 53*(2), 192-211.

References

Becker, W. E. & Johnston, C. (1999). The relationship between multiple choice and essay response questions in assessing economics understanding. *Economic Record, 75*(4), 348-357.

Bennett, R. E., Ward, W. C., Rock, D. A., & LaHart, C. (1990). Toward a framework for constructed-response items. *ETS Reseach Report N. 90-7.* Princeton, NJ: Educational Testing Service.

Birenbaum, M. & Tatuoka, K. K. (1987). Open-ended versus multiple-choice response formats- It does make a difference for diagnostic purposes. *Applied Psychological Measurement, 11*(4), 385-395.

Bloom, B. (1984). *Taxonomy of educational objectives, book i: Cognitive domain,* (2nd edition). New York: Addison Wesley Publishing Company.

Bloom, B. S., Englehart, M. D., Hill, W. H., Furst, E. J., & Krathwohl, D. R. (1956). *Taxonomy of educational objectives: The classification of educational goals, handbook i: Cognitive domain.* New York: Longmans, Green and Co.

Bonniol, J. J., Caverni, J. P., & Noizet, G. (1972). Le statut scolaire des eleves comme determinant de l'evaluation des devoirs qu'ils produisent. *Cahiers de Psychologie, 15*(12), 83-92.

Boynton, M. (1950). Inclusion of "none of these" makes spelling items more difficult. *Educational and Psychological Measurement, 10,* 431-432.

Breland, H. M. (1987). *Assessing writing skill. Research Monograph No. 11.* New York: College Board Publications.

Bridgeman, B. & Lewis, C. (1994). The relationship of essay and multiple-choice scores with grades in college courses. *Journal of Educational Measurement, 31*(1), 37-50.

Bridgeman, B., Morgan, R., & Wang, M. M. (1996). Choice among essay topics: Impact on performance and validity. *ETS Research Report Series, 1996*(1), i-22.

Briggs, D. (1970). The influence of handwriting on assessment. *Educational Research, 13*(1), 50-55.

Brimi, H. M. (2011). Reliability of grading high school work in English. *Practical Assessment, Research & Evaluation, 16*(7). Available online: http://pareonline.net/getvn.asp?v=16&n=17.

Brown, W. (1910). Some experimental results in the correlation of mental abilities. *British Journal of Psychology, 3,* 296-322.

References

Brozo, W. G., Schmelzer, R. V., & Spires, H. A. (1984). A study of test-wiseness clues in college and university teacher-made tests with implications for academic assistance centers. *College Reading and Learning Assistance Technical Report 84-01.*

Bull, R. & Stevens, J. (1979). The effects of attractiveness of writer and penmanship on essay grades. *Journal of Occupational Psychology, 52*(1), 53-59.

Calfee, R. C. & Miller, R. G. (2007). Best practices in writing assessment. In S. Graham, C. MacArthur & J. Fitzgerald (Eds.), *Best practices in writing instruction* (pp. 265-286). New York: Guilford Press.

Carter, K. (1986). Test-wiseness for teachers and students. *Educational Measurement: Issues and Practice 5*(4), 20-23.

Case, S. M. & Swanson, D. B. (1993). Extended-matching items: A practical alternative to free-response questions. *Teaching and Learning in Medicine: An International Journal, 5*(2), 107-115.

Case, S. M. & Swanson, D. B. (1998). *Constructing written test questions for the basic and clinical sciences.* Philadelphia, PA: National Board of Medical Examiners.

Cassels, J. R. T. & Johnstone, A. H. (1984). The effect of language on student performance on multiple choice tests in chemistry. *Journal of Chemical Education, 61,* 613-615.

Center for Educational Innovation, University of Minnesota. (2015). *General steps in test construction.* Retrieved on October 14, 2015, from http://cei.umn.edu/general-steps-test-construction.

Center for Innovation in Teaching and Learning, University of Illinois at Urbana-Champaign. (2016). *Assigning course grades.* Retrieved on February 12, 2016, from http://cte.illinois.edu/testing/exam/course_grades.html.

Chase, C. I. (1964). Relative length of option and response set in multiple choice items. *Educational and Psychological Measurement, 24,* 861-866.

Chase, C. I. (1968). The impact of some obvious variables on essay test scores. *Journal of Educational Measurement, 5*(4), 315-318.

Chase, C. I. (1979). The impact of achievement expectations and handwriting quality on scoring essay tests. *Journal of Educational Measurement, 16*(1), 39-42.

References

Clark, E. L. (1956). General response pattern to five-choice items. *Journal of Educational Psychology, 47*(2), 110-117.

Crehan, K. & Haladyna, T. M. (1991). The validity of two item-writing rules. *The Journal of Experimental Education, 59*(2), 183-192.

Cronbach, L. J. (1942). Studies of acquiescence as a factor in the true-false test. *Journal of Educational Psychology, 33*(6), 401.

Cronbach, L. J. (1946). Response sets and test validity. *Educational and Psychological Measurement, 6*(4), 475-494.

Cronbach, L. J. (1951). Coefficient alpha and the internal structure of tests. *Psychometrika, 16*(3), 297-334.

Crooks, T. J. (1988). The impact of classroom evaluation practices on students. *Review of Educational Research, 58,* 438-481.

Dalbert, D., Schneidewing, U., & Saalbach, A. (2007). Justice judgments concerning grading in school. *Contemporary Educational Psychology, 32*(3), 420-433.

Davis, L. (2015). The influence of training and experience on rater performance in scoring spoken language. *Language Testing,* doi: 0265532215582282.

DeMars, C. E. (2008). Scoring multiple choice items: A comparison of IRT and classical polytomous and dichotomous methods. In *Annual Meeting of the National Council of Measurement in Education,* New York.

DeVellis, R. F. (2012). *Scale development: Theory and applications* (Vol. 26). Los Angeles: Sage Publications.

Diekhoff, G. M., LaBeff, E. E., Clark, R. E., Williams, L. E., Francis, B., & Haines, V. J. (1996). College cheating: Ten years later. *Research in Higher Education, 37*(4), 487-502.

Dolly, J. P. & Williams, K. S. (1986). Using test-taking strategies to maximize multiple choice test scores. *Educational and Psychological Measurement, 46*(3), 619-625.

Downing, S. M. (2006). Selected-response item formats in test development. In S. M. Downing & T. M. Haladyna (Eds.) *Handbook of test development* (pp. 287-301). New York: Routledge.

Downing, S. M., Baranowski, R. A., Grosso, L. J., & Norcini, J. J. (1995). Item type and cognitive ability measured: The validity evidence for multiple true-false items in medical specialty certification. *Applied Measurement in Education, 8*(2), 187-207.

References

Dudycha, A. L. & Carpenter, J. B. (1973). Effects of item format on item discrimination and difficulty. *Journal of Applied Psychology, 58*(1), 116-121.

Dufresne, R. J., Leonard, W. J., & Gerace, W. J. (2002). Making sense of students' answers to multiple-choice questions. *The Physics Teacher, 40,* 174-180.

Dunn, T. F. & Goldstein, L. G. (1959). Test difficulty, validity, and reliability as functions of selected multiple choice item construction principles. *Educational and Psychological Measurement, 19,* 171-179.

Eisley, M. E. (1990). *The effect of sentence form and problem scope in multiple-choice item stems on indices of test and item quality.* Unpublished doctoral dissertation, Brigham Young University, Provo, UT.

Epstein, M. L., Lazarus, A. D., Calvano, T. B., & Matthews, K. A. (2002). Immediate feedback assessment technique promotes learning and corrects inaccurate first responses. *The Psychological Record, 52*(2), 187.

Evans, W. E. (1984). Test wiseness: An examination of cue-using strategies. *The Journal of Experimental Education, 52*(3), 141-144.

Faculty Center for Teaching and Learning, University of Central Florida. (2015). *Assessments.* Retrieved on October 14, 2015 at http://www.fctl.ucf.edu/TeachingAndLearningResources/LearningEnvironments/TeachingOnline/assessments.php.

Fenderson, B. A., Damjanov, I., Robeson, M. R., Veloski, J. J., & Rubin, E. (1997). The virtues of extended matching and uncued tests as alternatives to multiple choice questions. *Human Pathology, 28*(5), 526-532.

Fleming, M. & Chambers, B. A. (1983). Teacher-made tests: Windows on the classroom. *New Directions for Testing & Measurement, 19,* 29-38.

Forsyth, R. A. & Spratt, K. F. (1980). Measuring problem solving ability in mathematics with multiple-choice items: The effect of item format on selected item and test characteristics. *Journal of Educational Measurement, 17*(1), 31-43.

Frary, R. B. (1991). The none-of-the-above option: An empirical study. *Applied Measurement in Education, 4*(2), 115-124.

Frederiksen, N., Mislevy, R. J., & Bejar, I. I. (Eds.). (2012). *Test theory for a new generation of tests.* New York: Routledge.

References

Frederiksen, N. & Satter, G. A. (1953). The construction and validation of an arithmetical computation test. *Educational and Psychological Measurement, 13,* 209-227.

Frisbie, D. A. (1974). The effect of item format on reliability and validity: A study of multiple choice and true-false achievement tests. *Educational and Psychological Measurement, 34*(4), 885-892.

Frisbie, D. A. & Becker, D. F. (1991). An analysis of textbook advice about true-false tests. *Applied Measurement in Education, 4*(1), 67-83.

Fuchs, L. S. & Fuchs, D. (2001). Helping teachers formulate sound testing accommodation decisions for students with learning disabilities. *Learning Disabilities: Research & Practice, 16,* 174-181.

Gardner, W. M., Roper, J. T., Gonzalez, C. C., & Simpson, R. G. (1988). Analysis of cheating on academic assignments. *The Psychological Record, 38*(4), 543.

Green, K. (1984). Effects of item characteristics on multiple-choice item difficulty. *Educational and Psychological Measurement, 44*(3), 551-561.

Gross, L. J. (1994). Logical versus empirical guidelines for writing test items: The case of "none of the above." *Evaluation & the Health Professions, 17,* 123-126.

Guskey, T. R. (2006). "It wasn't fair!" Educators' recollections of their experiences as students with grading. Paper presented at the *Annual Meeting of the American Educational Research Association.*

Haladyna, T. M. (1999). *Developing and validating multiple choice test items,* (2nd ed). Mahwah: NJ: Lawrence Erlbaum Associates.

Haladyna, T. M. & Downing, S. M. (1989). Validity of a taxonomy of multiple choice item-writing rules. *Applied Measurement in Education, 2*(1), 51-78.

Haladyna, T. M. & Downing, S. M. (1993). How many options is enough for a multiple choice test item? *Educational and Psychological Measurement, 53*(4), 999-1010.

Haladyna, T. M. & Downing, S. M. (2004). Construct-irrelevant variance in high-stakes testing. *Educational Measurement: Issues and Practice, 23*(1), 17-27.

References

Haladyna T. M., Downing, S. M., & Rodriguez, M. C. (2002). A review of multiple choice item-writing guidelines for classroom assessment. *Applied Measurement in Education, 15(3),* 309-334.

Haladyna, T. M. & Rodriguez, M. (2013). *Developing and validating test items.* New York: Routledge.

Hancock, G. R., Thiede, K. W., Sax, G., & Michael, W. B. (1993). Reliability of comparably written two-option multiple choice and true-false test items. *Educational and Psychological Measurement, 53*(3), 651-660.

Harris, D. K. & Changas, P. S. (1994). Revision of Palmore's second facts on aging quiz from a true-false to a multiple choice format. *Educational Gerontology, 20*(8), 741-754.

Heim, A. W. & Watts, K. P. (1967). An experiment on multiple-choice versus open-ended answering in a vocabulary test. *British Journal of Educational Psychology, 37*(3), 339-346.

Hogan, T. P. & Murphy, G. (2007). Recommendations for preparing and scoring constructed-response items: What the experts say. *Applied Measurement in Education, 20*(4), 427-441.

Huesman, R. L. & Frisbie, D. A. (2000). The validity of ITBS reaching comprehension test scores for learning disabled and non-learning disabled students under extended-time conditions. Paper presented at the *Annual Meeting of the National Council on Measurement in Education,* New Orleans, LA.

Hughes, C. A., Salvia, J., & Bott, D. (1991). The nature and extent of test-wiseness cues in seventh- and tenth-grade classroom tests. *Assessment for Effective Intervention, 16*(2-3), 153-163.

Hughes, D. C., Keeling, B., & Tuck, B. F. (1983). Effects of achievement expectations and handwriting quality on scoring essays. *Journal of Educational Measurement, 20*(1), 65-70.

Hughes, H. H. & Trimble, W. E. (1965). The use of complex alternatives in multiple choice items. *Educational and Psychological Measurement, 25,* 117-126.

Huntley, R. M. & Plake, B. S. (1988). An investigation of multiple-response-option multiple choice items: Item performance and processing demands. Abstract retrieved from eric.ed.gov/?id=ED306236 on November 19, 2014.

Jones, P. D. & Kaufman, G. G. (1975). The differential formation of response sets by specific determiners. *Educational and Psychological Measurement, 35,* 821-833.

References

Jonsson, A. & Svingby, G. (2007). The use of scoring rubrics: Reliability, validity and educational consequences. *Educational Research Review, 2*(2), 130-144.

Kahneman, D. (2011). *Thinking, fast and slow.* New York: Macmillan.

Kaplan, R. M. & Saccuzzo, D. P. (2013). *Psychological testing and measurement: Principles, applications, and issues,* (8th ed). Belmont, CA: Wadsworth.

Kent, T. H., Jones, J. J., & Schmeiser, C. B. (1974). *Some rules and guidelines for writing multiple choice test items.* Iowa City: University of Iowa College of Medicine and American College Testing Program, 6.

King, K. V., Gardner, D. A., Zucker, S., & Jorgensen, M. A. (2004). The distractor rationale taxonomy: Enhancing multiple choice items in reading and mathematics. *Assessment Report.* New York: Pearson.

Kline, P. (2000). *The handbook of psychological testing* (2nd ed.), (p. 13). London: Routledge.

Knowles, S. L. & Welch, C. A. (1992). A meta-analytic review of item discrimination and difficulty in multiple choice items using "none-of-the-above". *Educational and Psychological Measurement, 52*(3), 571-577.

Kubiszyn, T. & Borich, G. (2010). *Educational testing and measurement: Classroom application and practice.* New York: John Wiley & Sons, Inc.

Lord, F. (1952). *A theory of test scores* (Psychometric Monograph No. 7). Richmond, VA: Psychometric Corporation. Retrieved from http://www.psychometrika.org/journal/online/MN07.pdf.

Lord, F. M. (1977). Optimal number of choices per item—A comparison of four approaches. *Journal of Educational Measurement, 14*(1), 33-38.

Lowman, J. (1984). *Mastering the techniques of teaching.* San Francisco, CA: Jossey-Bass.

Markham, L. R. (1976). Influences of handwriting quality on teacher evaluation of written work. *American Educational Research Journal, 13*(4), 277-283.

Marshall, J. C. & Powers, J. M. (1969). Writing neatness, composition errors, and essay grades. *Journal of Educational Measurement, 6*(2), 97-101.

References

McCabe, D. L. (1992). The influence of situational ethics on cheating among college students. *Sociological Inquiry, 62*(3), 365-374.

McCabe, D. L. & Pavela, G. (2004). Ten (updated) principles of academic integrity: How faculty can foster student honesty. *Change: The Magazine of Higher Learning, 36*(3), 10-15.

McDaniel, M. A., Roediger, H. L., & McDermott, K. B. (2007). Generalizing test-enhanced learning from the laboratory to the classroom. *Psychonomic Bulletin & Review, 14*(2), 200-206.

McMorris, R. F., Brown, J. A., Snyder, G. W., & Pruzek, R. M. (1972). Effects of violating item construction principles. *Journal of Educational Measurement, 9*(4), 287-295.

McNamara, W. J. & Weitzman, E. (1945). The effect of choice placement on the difficulty of multiple choice questions. *Journal of Educational Psychology, 36*(2), 103-113.

Metfessel, N. S. & Sax, G. (1958). Systematic biases in keying of correct responses on certain standardized tests. *Educational and Psychological Measurement, 18*, 787-790.

Millman, J., Bishop, C. H., & Ebel, R. (1965). An analysis of test-wiseness. *Educational and Psychological Measurement, 25*(3), 707-726.

Minstrell, J. (2000). Student thinking and related assessment: Creating a facet based learning environment. In N. S. Raju, J. W. Pellegrino, M. W. Bertenthal, K. J. Mitchell, & L. R. Jones (Eds.) *Grading the nation's report card: Research from the evaluation of NAEP* (pp. 44-73). Washington, DC: The National Academies Press.

Mosier, C. I. & Price, H. G. (1945). The arrangement of choices in multiple choice questions and a scheme for randomizing choice. *Educational and Psychological Measurement, 5*(4), 379-382.

Mueller, D. J. (1975). An assessment of the effectiveness of complex alternatives in multiple choice achievement test items. *Educational and Psychological Measurement, 35*, 135-141.

Oosterhof, A. C. & Glasnapp, D. R. (1974). Comparative reliabilities and difficulties of the multiple choice and true-false formats. *The Journal of Experimental Education, 42*(3), 62-64.

Osterlind, S. J. (1989). *What is constructing test items?* Netherlands: Springer.

References

Parkes, J., Fix, T. K., & Harris, M. B. (2003). What syllabi communicate about assessment in college classrooms. *Journal on Excellence in College Teaching, 14*(1), 61-83.

Peterson, C. C. & Peterson, J. L. (1976). Linguistic determinants of the difficulty of true-false test items. *Educational and Psychological Measurement, 36*(1), 161-164.

Pigge, F. L. & Marso, R. N. (1988). Supervisors agenda: Identifying and alleviating teachers' test construction errors. Paper presented at the *Annual Conference of the Ohio Association for Supervision and Curriculum Development.*

Plake, B. S. & Huntley, R. M. (1984). Can relevant grammatical cues result in invalid test items? *Educational and Psychological Measurement, 44,* 687-696.

Poundstone, W. (2014). *Rock breaks scissors: A practical guide to outguessing and outwitting almost everybody.* New York: Little, Brown and Company.

Putman, B. (2015) *Study smarter workshop: Study and test taking strategies.* Retrieved on July 21, 2015 from https://pages.southwestncc.edu/aca111wc/public/study_skills/.

Pyrczak, F. (1973). Use of similarities between stems and keyed choices in multiple-choice items. Paper presented at the *Annual Meeting of the National Council for Measurement in Education.*

Rezaei, R. & Lovorn, M. (2010). Reliability and validity of rubrics for assessment through writing. *Assessing Writing, 15*(1), 18-39.

Rimland, B. (1960a). The effect of including extraneous numerical information in a test of arithmetic reasoning. *Educational and Psychological Measurement, 20,* 787-794.

Rimland, B. (1960b). The effects of varying time limits and using "right answer not given" in experimental forms of the U.S. Navy Arithmetic Test. *Educational and Psychological Measurement, 20,* 533-539.

Rodriguez, M. C. (2005). Three options are optimal for multiple-choice items: A meta-analysis of 80 years of research. *Educational Measurement: Issues and Practice, 24*(2), 3-13.

Rossi, J. S., McCrady, B. S., & Paolino, Jr., T. J. (1978). A and B but not C: Discriminating power of grouped alternatives. *Psychological Reports, 42,* 1346.

Saltzman, J. (2007, October 7). Student takes his C to federal court: Judge dismisses suit against UMass. *The Boston Globe.*

References

Retrieved from
http://www.boston.com/news/education/higher/articles/2007/
10/04/student_takes_his_c_to_federal_court/?page=full.

Sarnacki, R. E. (1979). An examination of test-wiseness in the cognitive test domain. *Review of Educational Research, 49*(2), 252-279.

Schmeiser, C. B. & Whitney, D. R. (1973). The effect of selected poor item-writing practices on test difficulty, reliability and validity: A replication. Paper presented at the *Annual Meeting of the American Educational Research Association.*

Schmeiser, C. B. & Whitney, D. R. (1975). The effect of incomplete stems and "none of the above" foils on test and item characteristics. Paper presented at the *Annual Meeting of the National Council on Measurement in Education,* Washington, DC.

Schrock, T. J. & Mueller, D. J. (1982). Effects of violating three multiple-choice item construction principles. *The Journal of Educational Research, 75*(5), 314-318.

Scouller, K. (1998). The influence of assessment method on students' learning approaches: Multiple choice question examination versus assignment essay. *Higher Education, 35,* 453-472.

Semko, J. A. & Hunt, R. (2013). Legal matters in test security. In J. A. Wollack & J. J. Fremer (Eds.) *Handbook of test security.* New York: Routledge, 237-258.

Sireci, S. G., Scarpati, S. E., & Li, S. (2005). Test accommodations for students with disabilities: An analysis of the interaction hypothesis. *Review of Educational Research, 75,* 457-490.

Sireci, S. G., Wiley, A., & Keller, L. A. (1998). An empirical evaluation of selected multiple choice item writing guidelines. Paper presented at the *Annual Meeting of the Northeastern Educational Research Association.*

Smith, J. K. (1982). Converging on correct answers: A peculiarity of multiple choice items. *Journal of Educational Measurement, 19*(3), 211-220.

Solano-Flores, G. & Li, M. (2009). Generalizability of cognitive interview-based measures across cultural groups. *Educational Measurement: Issues and Practice, 28*(2), 9-18.

Spearman, C. C. (1910). Correlation calculated from faulty data. *British Journal of Psychology, 3,* 271-295.

References

Srinivasa, D. K. & Adkoli, B. V. (1989). Multiple choice questions: How to construct and how to evaluate? *Indian Journal of Pediatrics*, *56*, 69-74.

Strang, H. R. (1977). The effects of technical and unfamiliar options on guessing on multiple choice test items. *Journal of Educational Measurement*, *14*(3), 253-260.

Struyven, K., Dochy, F., & Janssens, S. (2005). Students' perceptions about evaluation and assessment in higher education: A review. *Assessment & Evaluation in Higher Education*, *30*(4), 325-341.

Tamir, P. (1993). Positive and negative multiple choice items: How different are they? *Studies in Educational Evaluation*, *19*(3), 311-325.

Tarrant, M., Ware, J., & Mohammed, A. M. (2009). An assessment of functioning and non-functioning distractors in multiple choice questions: A descriptive analysis. *BMC Medical Education*. Retrieved January 22, 2016. http://mbcmededuc.biomedcentral.com/articles/10.1186/1472-6920-9-40.

Tollefson, N. (1987). A comparison of the item difficulty and item discrimination of multiple choice items using the "none of the above" and one correct response options. *Educational and Psychological Measurement*, *47*(2), 377-383.

Traub, R. E. & Fisher, C. W. (1977). On the equivalence of constructed-response and multiple-choice tests. *Applied Psychological Measurement*, *1*(3), 355-369.

Tripp, A. & Tollefson, N. (1985). Are complex multiple choice options more difficult and discriminating than conventional multiple choice options? *Journal of Nursing Education*, *24*(3), 92-98.

Varma, S. (2006). *Preliminary item statistics using point-biserial correlation and p-values.* Morgan Hill CA: Educational Data Systems, Inc.

Vegada, B. N., Karelia, B. N., & Pillai, A. (2014). Reliability of four-response type multiple choice questions of pharmacology summative tests of II M.B.B.S students. *International Journal of Mathematics and Statistics Invention*, *2*(1), 6-10.

Wainer, H. & Thissen, D. (1993). Combining multiple-choice and constructed-response test scores: Toward a Marxist theory of test construction. *Applied Measurement in Education*, *6*, 103-118.

References

Walstad, W. B. & Becker, W. E. (1994). Achievement differences on multiple-choice and essay tests in economics. *American Economic Review, 84*(2), 193-196.

Waltman, K. K. & Frisbie, D. A. (1994). Parents' understanding of their children's report card grades. *Applied Measurement in Education, 7*(3), 223-240.

Ward, W. C. (1982). A comparison of free-response and multiple-choice forms of verbal aptitude tests. *Applied Psychological Measurement, 6*(1), 1-11.

Wedell, D. H., Parducci, A., & Roman, D. (1989). Student perceptions of fair grading: A range-frequency analysis. *The American Journal of Psychology,* 233-248.

Weiten, W. (1982). Relative effectiveness of single and double multiple choice questions in educational measurement. *The Journal of Experimental Education, 51*(1), 46-50.

Weiten, W. (1984). Violation of selected item construction principles in educational measurement. *The Journal of Experimental Education, 52*(3), 174-178.

Wesman, A. G. & Bennett, G. K. (1946). The use of "none of these" as an option in test construction. *Journal of Educational Psychology, 37*(9), 541-549.

Wevrick, L. (1962). Response set in a multiple-choice test. *Educational and Psychological Measurement, 22*(3), 533-538.

Williams, J. J. & Griffiths, T. L. (2013). Why are people bad at detecting randomness? A statistical argument. *Journal of Experimental Psychology: Learning, Memory, and Cognition, 39*(5), 1473-1490.

Williamson, M. L. & Hopkins, K. D. (1967). The use of "none-of-these" versus homogeneous alternatives on multiple-choice tests: Experimental reliability and validity comparisons. *Journal of Educational Measurement, 4*(2), 53-58.

Index

Made in the USA
Columbia, SC
15 April 2023

15409791R00128